Conrad (C+RAD) Martinez

Athruzy
of GOoD Humor
Poetry

GOoD Humor 101

WESTBOW
PRESS®
A DIVISION OF THOMAS NELSON
& ZONDERVAN

Front cover picture: Joseph Niehus at website (jpnphoto.com)

WestBow Press books may be ordered through booksellers or by contacting:

WestBow Press
A Division of Thomas Nelson & Zondervan
1663 Liberty Drive
Bloomington, IN 47403
www.westbowpress.com
1 (866) 928-1240

ISBN: 978-1-4908-7903-1 (sc)
ISBN: 978-1-4908-7904-8 (hc)
ISBN: 978-1-4908-7902-4 (e)

Library of Congress Control Number: 2015907308

Print information available on the last page.

WestBow Press rev. date: 07/14/2015

Dedication

This book is first dedicated to my Lord and Savior Jesus; who saw me through all of my life's work in progress situations. To my first mother Lily K Martinez (Manuela); my second mother Elizabeth Ann Martinez (Ortega: step-mother), My children; Anthony Nunez (step-son), Daughters: Lily K. Martinez (Torres), Leilani Lynn Martinez (Ramirez), Arianna Luz Martinez (deceased), Bethany Marie Martinez, and Conrad E Martinez (son).

Poetry101 1A

Oh, once upon a time, you just might say,
Oh, yes, once upon a time in a very fine way,
Life way back when was so simple and true.
Every day there was always something to do:
Walking to school with some neighborhood friends;
Just make it in time before the second bell ends.

Oh, how life is so simple through the eyes of an innocent child.
Oh, how life is so simple. It made living it worthwhile.

Days and nights in the very many hours of play,
Days and nights, a voice yelling to get home right away.
"Supper is ready," our parents would always say.
We held hands in giving God thanks, and we prayed.
Before going back out to play, better finish all your food.
Growing up in a family, this is what you had to do.

Oh, how life is so simple through the eyes of an innocent child.
Oh, how life is so simple. It made living it worthwhile.

I am much older now, with some wisdom and joy from above.
I am much older and, still with Jesus, rest assured of His love.
I've been blessed, very blessed, since He came into my life.
He's my Good Shepherd, guiding me from a life full of strife.
I will continue to praise Him for giving me parents whom I love
Until I see Him face-to-face, He who waits for me above.

Oh, how life is so simple through the eyes of an innocent child.
Oh, how life is so simple. It made living it worthwhile.

C+RAD

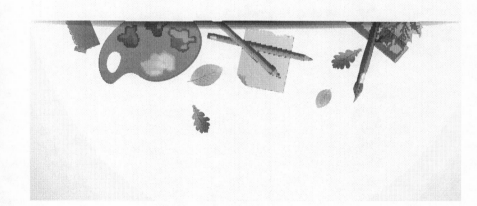

PoetryI0I IB

Here I gaze upon a clear, dark sky,
The man in the moon gleaming ever so high,
Like a cool, sleek gent struttin' down the street
With the Milky Way and stars at his feet.

The air is still, yet cool to the touch.
It is clear enough to see the other planets blush.
Saturn has its rings, and Mars always red,
Mercury and Jupiter I think went to bed

How often moonbeams shine down with delight.
You can wish upon a star almost every night.
Seeing is believing with the moon at your side.
All cares and worries seem to fly by.

As the dawn breaks and the moon turns in,
We see the silhouette of a very dear friend,
Until once again in a clear, dark sky
The man in the moon gleams ever so high.

C+RAD

Poetry101 1C

The piano—it may surprise you—anyone can play.
That piano may surprise you—go try it someday.
Ah, you may think, *I just don't have time.*
Consider this thought in a long grocery line.
So who, what, where, or how does one start?
Don't you worry. Just go with the beat of your heart.

Be it piano or any instrument you play,
Be it piano or any instruments, go and make someone's day.

Men, women, and children, even babies have tried.
From Washington to Obama, hey have they lied.
Okay, so you have some rhythm, and yet to feel the blues,
Hey, sooner or later you'll be playing in suede shoes.
If it takes lessons or DVDs to play them bones,
Then go, daddy, go, for me and Mrs. Jones.

Be it piano or any instrument you play,
Be it piano or any instruments, go and make someone's day.

Now you're rock in' and rollin' or Bach and Beethoven,
Let everyone hear what the heck you got goin'.
It may not sound like Elton, Joel, Lewis, or Gilley.
They call it the sound of music—go ahead, be silly.
Who knows; your music may reach and touch a person.
Music is also known to heal a heart when you listen.

Be it piano or any instrument you play,
Be it piano or any instrument, go and make someone's day

C+RAD

Poetry101 ID

Life in general with its ups and downs,
Is like an EKG monitor going to town.
Some areas of the world are very fast paced,
Many countries and cities fighting for first place.

Back in the day, life was slow and true.
Everyone made time to go to the zoo.
Freeways and side roads are packed like sardines,
Like young and old women with sprayed-on jeans.

Come on now, life; time to brake—you're moving too fast,
Even the steady climb of a gallon of gas.
The rich are getting richer and the poor even poorer.
The United States was known for the great, mighty dollar.

Now I pose a question, whether rhyme or not:
Are you happy with life and with things that mean a lot?
If not, Jesus is ready. He died and rose to heaven
For all young or old men, women, and children.

C+RAD

Poetry101 IE

A voice or song has led many to go wrong,
A voice or song, like a junk in Hong Kong.
Now let me see; well, better yet, let me listen
To uncensored, polluted, and unadulterated suggestions,
Where bad is good and good is bad.
Almost gone are the morals this world once had.

Over two thousand years ago, a man died for our shame.
Over two thousand years ago; more than a man—Jesus is His name.

Stopped at a red light, paltry music playing nearby.
Stopped at a red light, now my turn to go bye-bye.
Music and lyrics have changed or evolved,
Pretty much hand to hand, such as Peter and Paul.
So stop if you want no more rhyme with reason.
There is one true voice; we all need to listen.

Over two thousand years ago, a man died for our shame.
Over two thousand years ago; more than a man—Jesus is His name.

He created you and me to be obedient and free.
He created you and me; now we are humbled to our knees.
How can something good turn around and change to bad?
When a voice or song introduces a bad plan,
The world says that life is a circus. This maybe.
The Word of life came to set all people free.

Over two thousand years ago, a man died for our shame.
Over two thousand years ago; more than a man—Jesus is His name.

C+RAD

Poetry101 IF

"To err is only human," we may justify and say.
"Not in the very beginning," the Word spoke that day.
We fight, shun one another, and won't even get along.
Hey, Lucifer and a third from heaven chose to do wrong.

Have we all forgotten we're created in His image?
Oops, we mistakenly gave up our heavenly privilege.
Life can be really rough when in sinking sand.
Please remember that we're created and He's the man.

Time will tell of choices we have made.
Some live life like a game of charades.
Laugh or cry if all this is true.
We are all sinners who need to know what to do.

His name is Jesus—God, man, son of David.
The Son of God, a sinless life He truly lived.
Believe in Him, the spotless Lamb. He died for me and you.
Yes, we as humans, this is what we must do.

C+RAD

Poetry101 IG

"A penny for your thoughts," was the coined phrase to say.
A penny for your thoughts has gone up in price today.
This ol' world, as we know, is not growing any larger,
Won't accept nothin' greater than a bill of twenty dollars.
It's sad to see the economy all around decline
As prices and the nation's debt continue to climb.

Is there a price or value for your soul to pay?
Is there a price or value? Yes, Jesus paid it all the way.

There are more cars on the road than dairy cows in the field.
There are more cars than oil the Valdez tanker spilled.
Come on now, everyone. We are living way beyond our need.
I agree it takes a two-income family to support all capitalist greed.
Then when I see our country's principles and freedoms turned away,
That is when we the people should be humbled and should pray.

Is there a price or value for your soul to pay?
Is there a price or value? Yes, Jesus paid it all the way.

I know that as a nation we are all smarter than a fifth grader.
I know that as a nation we need to turn to the one and only Creator.
Since the fall of man, we are still dancing with two left feet,
Like a rowboat without paddles trying to go up a creek.
A great nation can only be one governed by heavenly oracles.
As a nation we are illiterate in sixty-six principles.

Is there a price or value for your soul to pay?
Is there a price or value? Yes, Jesus paid it all the way.

C+RAD

PoetryI0I IH

Having children is a blessing to some and to others a nightmare;
Decision and planning or simply two people losing their underwear.
Don't be pointing fingers; remember, it takes two to tango.
It takes a captain to guide a ship and a pilot to touch and go.

As adorable little babies, they just eat, sleep, and poop.
Soon they will grow, wanting Cheerios or even a Fruit Loop.
It's really amazing how they like imitating our every action.
As we grow older, it will be they helping us with fractions.

Let us now remind ourselves of this most valuable treasure to give.
This treasure is also found in all hearts wanting to live.
They're only on loan to us for a season to witness the love and care.
This love came in the form of a babe God gave us to love and share.

Now, lest we forget, written in the Bible, the first two kids, Cain and Abel,
A real, true-life story, and for sure not some made-up fairy tale.
Yes, we as parents will be held responsible, whether good or bad,
For all the big and little kids of this world that we all once had.

C+RAD

Poetry101 Ii

Life and death we all share; that is true.
Life and death can make you turn a shade of blue.
Compared to Yin and Yang or love and hate,
Good and bad choices we all tend to make
This is life; to enjoy it one day at a time,
live simple and free in newness of springtime.

Jesus conquered death and the grave; now we are free.
Jesus conquered death and the grave; yes this He did for you and me.

Death shuns life, has no regard whether young or old.
Death shuns life, yet there is a place with streets of gold.
The ignorant and weak-minded cannot conceive of such a place.
Pride will rob anyone from turning their heart to a saving grace.
Life and death each hold a significant worth or value.
Regardless of your status in life, the choice is up to you.

Jesus conquered death and the grave; now we are free.
Jesus conquered death and the grave; yes, this He did for you and me.

God bless America, the land that I truly love.
God bless America; send us your peace from above.
Turn our heart back and make us a God-fearing nation.
Remind and refresh us toward your great salvation.
Let this be in our heart and mind to be ready.
Never fear the Grim Reaper; Jesus holds the key to this day.

Jesus conquered death and the grave; now we are free.
Jesus conquered death and the grave; yes, this He did for you and me.

C+RAD

Poetry101 lj

Love and marriage match together like hand and glove,
Resonating purity that can only come from above,
More captivating than any rainbow Sony or Fuji could produce.
The author and matchmaker—His name in Spanish is Jesus.

Love, faith, hope—love is the greatest of the three.
To keep a marriage intact takes humbleness on our knee.
It takes dedication and work, like flying or landing a plane.
You don't want any monkey business; just ask Tarzan and Jane.

Since the beginning it's always been male and female.
Can't trust a government that relies only on appeals.
Boy it's so true prides goes before a fall.
Wisdom cries out, and no one listens at all.

The only one that can fix this is only the author.
Anyone else is just a fake make believer.
So as the world wrestles with its own downfall,
Put your trust and faith in the one who created all

C+RAD

Poetry101 IK

Time there is always never enough or too little of.
Time—you could be thanking your lucky stars above.
We wake up, go to lunch, and turn in for the day.
Oh, please excuse me; I just made a purchase on eBay.
It may seem as though there are more hours in a day.
We have done almost everything except read the Bible and pray.

Time and experience are the teachers of many things.
Time and life's choices don't wait, or the fat lady sings.

Time seems to fly by when you're out having fun.
Time seems to fly by come rain, snow, or sun.
You can be sure time will never be early or late.
Oh, better remember this on your very first date.
There has always been a beginning, and for sure there's an end.
What will happen after this life? Is heaven where you'll spend?

Time and experience are the teachers of many things.
Time and life's choices don't wait, or the fat lady sings.

Life is like grass that wilts and fades away.
Life is like a vapor you see but gone that day
So time keeps on rolling, ticking by; second, minute, and hour.
God said "I give my life for many and raise it up; I have the power."
So time is very precious to everyone, you see.
God took the time for us; do the same on your knee.

Time and experience are the teachers of many things.
Time and life's choices don't wait, or the fat lady sings.

C+RAD

Poetry101 IL

Putting on and then taking off the weight—
It's like two sumo wrestlers at a tea party: so great.
From the beginning to the very end of the year,
We promise and swear to trim down the rear.

TV or radio, even smart phone ads,
Try to lure you for a quick and easy plan.
For sure weight gain will not happen overnight,
Like ghouls, goblins, and zombies that come out at midnight.

Now remember, we're all different from head to toe,
Just like the three stooges: Curly, Larry, and Moe.
Think on this: mind over matter; and no pain, no gain.
We're not made like Superman, fit to stop a freight train.

We're all made in the image of our Creator.
There's a time at which our bodies will be changed for later.
He said to encourage one another because of His love,
To be ready every day for our true home above.

C+RAD

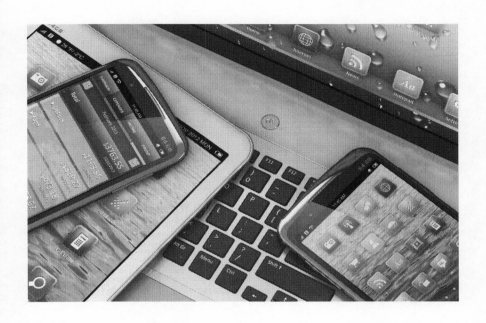

Poetry101 IM

There are times when things will just fall out of place.
There are times, it seems, you just need a little space.
Spit happens.
Start clappin'
Hey, who knows?
Say good-bye to your sorrows.

Count from one to ten.
Count, then do it again.

People are out there wanting to press your button.
People are out there just plain stinkin' doing nothin'.
So don't you worry.
Get yourself up early,
Wear that great smile,
Go another extra mile.

Count from one to ten.
Count, then do it again.

When people will have nothin' good to say,
When people ask for forgiveness then pray,
Shout with joy of heart.
God always does His part
From the beginning to end.
He'll always be your friend.

Count from one to ten.
Count, then do it again.

C+RAD

Poetry101 IN

Competition gave way to globalization all around, you see.
The boundaries have stretched far beyond sea to shining sea.
Competition didn't take away the mom-and-pop store.
Greed from humanistic government, it has everybody sore.

When governments cannot govern by their own laws,
Then we need Hanna-Barbera and Quick Draw McGraw.
I believe that everyone could use a helping hand,
Like Chico Rodriguez in *Chico and the Man*.

It is nothing new when governments rob from the very poor.
We're all human yet treat no one well anymore.
The world is turning into a no-holds-barred mind-set.
We have forgotten His name; this nation will soon regret.

Of the increase of His government and peace, there will be no end.
His arm is stretched out still, and willing to give a helping hand.
Where can such a government come from and truly exist?
From humans with heavenly principles in their hearts, who persist

C+RAD

Poetry101 10

Summer is leaving, it goes at a crawl.
Summer is leaving and soon turns to fall.
Summer has spent and for sure has gone by.
Bye-bye hot, humid air—oh, with a sigh.
Weather all around has changed a lot,
Like brother and sister and their dirty socks.

People change, though not like the seasons.
People change; God has the right reasons.

You name it, give it time, and certainly it will change.
You name it, like playing a very fun guessing game.
Change is something you like or not
When it goes your way and not what you thought.
So love it or leave;
There is nothin' up anyone's sleeve.

People change, though not like the seasons.
People change; God has the right reasons.

In the beginning, God gave man a command.
Man could not measure up to His plan.
This is what happens when changes take place,
When attitudes make us fall from His embracing grace.
His plan is the same; it sure hasn't changed.
Stop pointing a finger; it's us—we're to blame.

People change, though not like the seasons.
People change; God has the right reasons.

C+RAD

Poetry101 1P

Life is not fun when behind the eight ball.
Loud talking or yelling, not listening at all—
If words could cut, they would make you bleed.
His love minus self is all that we need.

There is loud talking but yet no meaning.
We wrestle and strive with too much feeling.
It's our character we have that needs to be checked.
His Word is a mirror; how does your image reflect?

Whether father, mother, daughter or son,
Don't let this eight ball weigh like a ton.
We need one another regardless of self.
Be like the blind man who yelled for help.

As we feed the body, the soul needs to be fed.
His Word gives clarity and self-control instead.
So the next time you're behind the eight ball,
Give God the glory and let Him do it all.

C+RAD

PoetryIOI IQ

Misunderstandings, yes, they happen quite often.
Misunderstandings—people will make something out of nothin'.
Mistakes will happen whether we like it or not.
Have you gone to buy something and then almost forgot?
Our brain can handle just so much information.
Like a bullet train slowing at a Metrolink station.

Our lives were made to live simple and free.
Our lives He holds with love for you and me.

Multitasking is the save-your-butt for the company.
Multitasking is great for the multiple personality.
There is nothin' new that hasn't been done under the sun.
Just a big revolving door; just do it to get it done.
We are still a primitive culture living in an outside-the-box mentality,
So get your head out of the TV box, TV show reality.

Our lives were made to live simple and free.
Our lives He holds with love for you and me.

Being human and misunderstandings are part of the cloth.
Being human, forgiving is surely needed a lot.
Seventy times seven—a golden rule of thumb.
You won't get indigestion or ever need a Tums.
True satisfaction is what this will bring.
"No satisfaction" is what this world sings.

Our lives were made to live simple and free.
Our lives He holds of love for you and me.

C+RAD

Poetry101 IR

The eyes are windows to the heart and soul,
Revealing a true character from head to toe—
Tall, short, light or heavy,
And drives a Dodge or Ford, please not a Chevy.

We're all made from a one-size-fits-all mold.
This mold has some worldly cracks; this I'm told.
Imperfections and flaws, now how can this be?
From disobedience and listening to a voice from a tree.

In this world, take care not to draw the short straw.
Then again, you might end up on the wrong side of the law.
Never had a date? Pray you don't go to jail.
You won't want to be some ones night' in gale

So how is your character? Is it bad? is it good?
What would you do different to change if you could?
It must come from the heart for this to take place.
God the Son made a way and gave us His grace.

C+RAD

Poetry101 IS

Laughter by far is the best medicine around.
Laughter—go ahead and laugh out loud
At home, or work, even if in school.
Sometimes we laugh when we're not suppose to.
Anyway, we laugh when it's just so funny.
Especially when one is like a dummy.

A sense of humor now and then,
A sense of humor with a silly grin.

Laugh and the world laughs with you.
Smile and people will smile back too.
We love to laugh and rib each other
Come rain or shine; it really doesn't matter.
Silent or modern movies of today
Slip in slapstick, all from yesterday.

A sense of humor now and then,
A sense of humor with a silly grin.

Don't let a nice smile end up being a frown
Let no one or anything try to put you down
Listen to or read something that is very inspirational.
Keep your heart and mind from doing the opposite you know.
Laugh humorously with those who have self-esteem.
God has humor; He made you—if you know what I mean.

A sense of humor now and then,
A sense of humor with a silly grin.

C+RAD

Poetry101 IT

Separation and divorce—which one's first?
Guys end up losing more than a shirt.
It's a lawyer-eat-lawyer type of world out there.
Don't be surprised to see your lawyer in underwear.

I'm trying not to be bias-ply; just had a blowout.
Emotions running high; can't figure things out.
Does it really matter, the duration of a marriage,
When it's all over and life is one big hemorrhage?

Marriage is like flying a kite, you see.
If not flown right, it'll end up in a tree,
Like pilots landing planes or captains landing ships in harbor.
A sense of worth you felt as you made your first dollar.

I give praise to God; He's done so much in my life.
Sure, there were times I missed my ex-wife.
Remember, spit happens to everyone, you see.
On His strength only we're able to bend a knee.

C+RAD

PoetryIOI IU

Politics and religion have disobedience all over.
Politics and religion sell out for mega dollars.
Don't ever mix politics and religion together.
Try to hold a skunk's nose not to let it smell forever.
Oil and vinegar, or lipstick on the collar—
One of the two will allure you by far.

Obedience, not sacrifice, is the name of the game.
Obedience, not sacrifice, will put you back on His plane.

Government and countries play the game of life.
Government and countries full of bitterness and strife.
World religion or political leaders
Need to curtail being all-around cheaters.
All world leaders remember the oath you spoke.
Major promises with fingers crossed were the real big joke.

Obedience, not sacrifice, is the name of the game.
Obedience, not sacrifice, will put you back on his plane.

A real true leader is one from the trenches.
A real true leader spends no time with promises.
This world would be a better place to live in.
Let's start from the top and add some heaven.
The one real reason why the world is the way it is—
Man was blindsided with the three-letter word called sin.

Obedience, not sacrifice, is the name of the game.
Obedience, not sacrifice, will put you back on his plane.

C+RAD

Poetry|0| IV

Halloween is known as a mixed bag of candy,
Also for ghoulish costumes, yet some looking quiet dandy.
Old favorites like Wolfman, Dracula, and don't forget Frankie—
Remember to recharge him, or he just might get cranky ("Aarr!").

Adults and teens, even babies too,
Go out to impress in their favorite costume.
Adults like kids, and kids like adults.
Good thing you don't see old people doing somersaults.

It's really amazing what this day does to people,
But it's only second to what goes on in a church steeple.
This day is known to bring darkness and evil
As people watch TV and scary movie sequels.

The days of Noah are soon coming to pass.
People's hearts grow evil oh so very fast.
This has to happen before it will be better.
God's Word states this in sixty-six letters.

C+RAD

Poetry101 IW

Death, to all, is an uninvited shadow.
Death to all will bring sadness and sorrow.
My condolence to those who have lost a loved one,
Like a day filled with despair and clouds hiding the sun.
Now a void only friends and family with love can truly fill,
With heartfelt thoughts and warm memories that thrill.

Don't say good-bye, just say hello.
Don't say good-bye, just say aloha.

We prepare for disasters that come from everywhere.
We should always be ready for a hope of heaven up there.
Yes, many things we spend on and try to make time for.
Do you remember or recall Christ knocking at your door?
Death, to any believer, is described only as a sting.
It will not or cannot hurt you if a son or daughter of the King.

Don't say good-bye, just say hello.
Don't say good-bye, just say aloha.

Twelve ordinary men who were with Christ died for what they believed in.
Twelve ordinary men are in heaven because of a dear true friend.
The world shows enmity to all who love and revere Christ,
Takes care of its very own full of evil and strife.
The trumpet sound is the calling to all saints everywhere.
Christ and His bride the church will soon meet in the air.

Don't say good-bye, just say hello.
Don't say good-bye, just say aloha.

C+RAD

Poetry101 IX

Life will grab or kick in those jewels,
Putting you to the test on what you're to do.
Hang on there, cowboy, busting a wild stallion.
Wait for it, wait for it; then it'll happen.

Yes, patience is needed in this here life's journey.
Trial and error, or better get to bed real early.
Better make sure you've covered your bases
Like a generator running on all its phases.

Blessed is the man that has his house in order.
Then there's the other man fleeing for the border.
We all deal with a crisis of something so differently,
But it sure makes a difference when on bended knee.

A man named Solomon asked God for wisdom.
God gave him wisdom to run a vast kingdom.
Help me; I pray for a country that lacks wisdom.
Then we can say liberty reigns, and also true freedom.

C+RAD

Poetry101 ly

What will drive you and motivate your day?
What better than a convertible cruising toward the bay?
Many products claim to quick-start your engine.
New scientific ingredients just too long to mention.
We rely on pharmaceutical rather than pure natural,
Having sure side effects, making the skin way too colorful.

A glimpse of heaven is all we need.
A glimpse of heaven will do, yes indeed.

A kind gesture, compliment, or maybe even a hug.
A kind gesture helps get your giddy-up get along.
Your perspective on how to get your get going
Helps you think things out with assurance and knowing.
It is good to have confidence each and everyday.
Problems will come and eventually go away.

A glimpse of heaven is all we need.
A glimpse of heaven will do, yes indeed.

In a world that's trying to get ahead of itself,
In a world where basic knowledge is collecting dust on a shelf,
We the people need to stop and smell some roses,
Go out on a ranch and giddy-up, ride some horses.
The sphere of this world is changing and looking like a box.
The darkness of man's state is terribly overwhelming a lot.

A glimpse of heaven is all we need.
A glimpse of heaven will do, yes indeed.

C+RAD

Poetry101 12

God the Father created the heavens and the earth.
His vast presence hovered around all things first.
He spoke, and light obeyed His solemn command.
Light and darkness He separated without lifting a hand.

Days one through five were created, and He called them good.
On day six He created you and me and said "Ah, very gut."
With love so unsurpassed, His image we all hold
More precious than rubies, diamonds, or even gold.

Day seven He saved for last for one very good reason.
Of course He created the first time-out before any sport season.
He also knew the importance of how to relax.
I hope we as humans can follow suit on that.

God has given me a tremendous love for poetry.
To have penned inspiring thoughts just noteworthy,
I stand amazed and in awe of how He showed me
The beauty and the love that is found in all poetry.

C+RAD

Poetry101

God's Gracious Love

God is more than gracious.
His love is very contagious,
A sense of humor that's outrageous
While molding me in many stages.
Sent His Son to save us—
That kind of love is humungous—
The God/man that walked among us.

C+RAD

Poetry101

God's Mercy Is Available

God's tender mercies are available
24-7 when our lives seem very unstable.
He cares when we're not very grateful,
All happening when we're a tad bit sinful.
His Son who gave His life, don't you know,
While loving you and me is very amiable,
Yet a world shunning His love is very awful.

C+RAD

Poetry101

Jesus Is God's Only Son

Jesus is the only Son of God
Who bore our sins, which left Him scarred.
Scarred, yet unselfish love embraced a world—
A world disturbed, not wanting to be purged.
He cried out loud "Forgive them, Father;
I give my life for You to honor;
To honor sinful hearts in becoming proper."

C+RAD

Poetry101

God's Thoughts and Ways

God's thoughts are higher, and His ways always better.
Better heavenly minded, not worrying about earthly treasures,
Treasures that can change a heart into many other pleasures,
Pleasures that will rob a soul into becoming a transgressor,
A transgressor who's in the need of a true loving Savior,
A loving Savior whose thoughts and ways are always better,
Better because of God's only Son, our High Priest and Savior.

C+RAD

Poetry101

The Word Is Our Treasure

Every believer's treasure is the wonderful Word of God
The Word that's changing sinful hearts already marred.
Jesus was marred taking the shame that sin had harbored,
Harbored, yet God looked down at His Son He has honored,
Honored in His Father's plans to rid sin He did conquer,
Conquered what the Devil thought could never be unconquered.
Conjured and awkward, the Devil chose to be dishonored.

C+RAD

Poetry101

God's Peace and Success

David, the son of Jesse, gladly took care of his father's sheep.
He would observe and learn from God on how to succeed.
Success God has for everyone with cares and daily needs
When we're humble as He strengthens all of our beliefs,
Giving room to breathe when going through some major griefs
When God is in control while comforting and giving peace
To an unforgiving world, which Jesus can and only brings.

C+RAD

Poetry101

My Meditations

Hear my words, O Lord, and consider my meditations.
My meditations bring me toward your gracious salvation,
Salvation to be enjoyed and accepted with all adorations,
Adorations of the heart bringing healings and restorations,
Restorations so complete without any limitations,
Limitations that have no restrictions, for you are the Lord Jesus,
The Lord Jesus, who restores lives strewn in many pieces.

C+RAD

The Lazy Man

As a door turns on hinges, so a lazy man turns in his bed,
A bed maybe of roses or thorns—which of the two instead?
Instead of happy or sad, what other mood would you accept?
Accept Jesus died for a world with love 100 percent.
100 percent pure and simple, this He did without any regrets.
Regrets only the Devil will have, and this he'll never forget,
Forgetting that he's created and will soon inherit one huge debt.

C+RAD

Poetry101

Who Can Find a Virtuous Wife?

Who can find a virtuous wife,
A wife you can enjoy with all your life,
A life together with our Savior, Jesus the Christ,
The Christ who brought life back to a world paralyzed?
He healed many without any sort of compromise.
A compromise from evil ways the Devil amplifies,
Amplifies our sinful nature only to scrutinize.

C+RAD

Poetry101

A Foolish Heart

He who trusts in his heart is a fool,

A fool who'll have a mind of a mule,

A mule God uses to show man is minuscule,

A minuscule still tooling around in preschool,

A preschool with basic fundamentals and many rules,

Rules that are needed to govern ungodly moods,

Moods that will try to curtail godly absolutes.

C+RAD

Poetry101

Evil Men

Don't be envious of evil men,

Evil men who become worthless conmen,

Conmen who are wolves dressed up as congressmen,

Congressmen who think they're funny comedians,

Comedians who have in humor sleaziness,

Sleaziness mixed with worldly disobedience,

Disobedience God took care of on a cross of obedience.

C+RAD

A True King's Heart

A King's heart is in the hand of the Lord,
The Lord who's from the tribe of Judah and well adored,
Adored for His Word, sharper than any double-edged sword,
A sword He's not afraid of using to bring order restored,
Restoring and thwarting all evil this world has absorbed,
Absorbed and implored; His beloved Son God has adorned,
Adorned to transform sinful hearts with His love outpoured.

C+RAD

PoetryIOI 2A

Boys and girls are cut from two very different cloths,
Boys and girls, having to change daily from dirty socks.
Kids are always growing so full of energy and zeal,
Like a pup chasing its tail or a seagoing pup seal.
Yes, the federal government needs to research this quality energy,
Whether bike riding, skateboarding, or just throwing a Frisbee.

Kids need to be kids, not miniature adults.
Kids need good moral role-models who love

Webelos, Brownies, scouts, and eagles—
Tremendous organizations with good moral appeals.
You can take an adult out from a kid, but not a kid out from adults.
This world would change for the better, wanting good moral results.
Take away all the high-paid TV show psychologists.
Reprimand kids' parents inside their high-dollar wallets.

Kids need to be kids, not miniature adults.
Kids need good moral role-models who love.

This is a moral degeneration biased on the slant of a world.
This was a moral republic country slowly dying; it once was herald.
Kids are the life blood if this world is to continue.
They need leaders with insight and heavenly principles.
The Word of God likens heaven to such as a precious child.
Pray with an open heart for this, and away with all denial.

Kids need to be kids, not miniature adults.
Kids need good moral role-models who love.

C+RAD

Poetry101 2B

High noon driving is sometimes just a waste of time.
Freeways and roads crowded in like a thin dime
The want to be hot rods—Hondas, Toyotas, and Nissans.
Sound like muffler-driven mowers, nothing really to rant on.

On ramps and off ramps, a mixture of red rover—red rover.
Hey people, please, I'm begging you to let me merge over.
With attitudes as big as Mt. Everest or Mt. Rainier,
Wild hogs and suicide rockets zoomin without fear.

Freeways and highways were a means to get places quicker,
Not to see if your car could break the world sound barrier.
Driving these days has taken on a different meaning,
Always in a rush with a hey-you-get-out-of-my-way feeling.

The world was created in seven days with joy, love, and fun.
Each day is considered a thousand years, or a thousand years as one.
God took the time with no deadlines and no pressure to rush.
Let us please take note of this with no rhyme or reason to fuss.

C+RAD

PoetryIOI 2C

Do you believe or doubt that the God of the Bible is truly real?
Do you even believe there's a devil out for your soul to steal?
One is the Creator and the other is a creation.
The Creator, He is the foremost and author of salvation.
He made everything in heaven, and also angelic beings.
He made man—though a little lower, if you know what I mean.

One is the Creator, and the other a counterfeit.
One has the Crown of Life and the Word to prove it.

The counterfeit—an archangel whose name was Lucifer.
This counterfeit's pride was found, now named the deceiver.
This Lucifer made a very wrong choice that cost him so severely.
One third of the heavenly Host sided and cost him quite dearly.
This deceiver doesn't allow or take any kind of hankering,
Will not allow anyone on or near the verge of believing.

One is the Creator, and the other a counterfeit.
One has the Crown of Life and the Word to prove it.

Now you choose what is good or bad and real or fake.
Now you choose willingly whom you'll have your soul to take.
God created you and me with His abundant love so tenderly.
The deceiver wants nothing more than you to bow your knee.
I pray that you choose very wisely, for this will last forever.
God has nothing but love for you; the deceiver—that's his nature.

One is the Creator, and the other a counterfeit.
One has the Crown of Life and the Word to prove it.

C+RAD

Poetry101 2D

The fall season has arrived; it's the season of yearly change.
Deciduous trees bare all just like adult websites doing the same.
Ah, cool quiescent air with low, thick, hazy gray clouds.
Fine misty drops falling won't let Mr. Sun come out.

The fall colors vivid and unusual, yet perfect for the season.
Now you have X amount of days to shop for all your reasons.
Baseball playoffs; yes, boo-hoo, the skies are gray in L.A.
It takes just three big owners to supply them with their pay.

There's just something about fall that will always bring the kid out.
Of course it's gridiron football, now go and let out a big shout.
Favorite team-logo rivalry and awesome tailgate parties;
It is all about having some fun on Saturday and Sun-fun-days.

I don't know about you, but I enjoy this time of the year.
It's a good time just to reflect with simplicity from ear to ear.
Jesus took the time and prayed for so many, don't you see.
Let us do the same for others as He did for you and me.

C+RAD

Poetry101 2E

To scribe on paper some reflections from real deep thought;
To scribe on paper some of life's reward bringing self-worth a lot.
Eloquence and intonation can move mountains if put to the test.
Just as a symphony conductor orchestrates brilliance when at his best.
Time and patience are the Rock of Gibraltar of foundations; this you'll see
From writing and rewriting with crumpled paper almost up to your knee.

Gusto and desire are what make scribing fly.
Gusto and desire—a marathon runner's ultimate high.

You'll be surprised how venting out emotions can and will help you.
You'll be surprised how many ways there are to lace up or tie your shoe.
Endurance is another factor in scribing things on paper.
Hours upon hours and nothing to show; just go on, and resume later.
Always the challenge is penning it right, giving your all every time,
To develop a skill—having free-flowing wit trickling inside your mind.

Gusto and desire are what make scribing fly.
Gusto and desire—a marathon runner's ultimate high.

When it is penned and you're completely done on each verse,
When it is penned and you're humming second-verse rhymes as the first,
Experiences in your life and willing to share are the gel that brings this together,
Like a captain returning from roaming the seas in good or bad sea weather.
Really it is all about having some fun and striving in being creative.
Remember, continue to pen with your heart, sharing all you can give.

Gusto and desire are what make scribing fly.
Gusto and desire—a marathon runner's ultimate high.

C+RAD

Poetry101 2F

Becoming a step takes on a Christlike love,
Showing everyone what you're really made up of.
Whether a father, mother, sister, or brother,
Time is the essence in loving one another.

It maybe that you'll bring something unique
To add to that family, making it as strong as concrete.
It may be a challenge—so what? What else is new?
That's what Christ did when He died for me and you.

So let there be no more a whining or a moaning
Because now your slip or underwear is a showing.
Take this advantage in filling this void or gap.
Go and show this family how you've learned to adapt.

Two-thousand years ago, a man died for me and you.
The world didn't receive His love, and He died of a broken heart too.
Death couldn't keep Him down; His love lifted Him on high.
He cried to the Father, "Forgive them," as the world yelled, "Crucify!"

C+RAD

PoetrylOl 2G

Human frailties have an attraction for the mind, soul, and body.
Human frailties yearn for the young and old in every society.
The mind is our source for intellect and cognitive reasoning.
So now you made it through the weekend from that terrible hangover feeling.
Your mind over matter says no way, but that mind won't matter is your thing.
So now for you it's okay and cool to be weird, silly, or a ding-O-ling.

Our bodies were made to last forever; then sin came and ruined the picture.
Our bodies were made not for the grave. Christ died; He arose and lives forever.

The soul may differ from person to person whether a moral or emotional nature.
The soul will take on human nature and strive to become like a creature.
Everyone should know they have a soul, depending on what foot you start with.
The soul is able to do good or bad on what you wish to accomplish.
Your soul is your character, so be yourself; there is only one of you.
Your soul is precious in the eyes of God. Trust Him; He'll see you through.

Our bodies were made to last forever; then sin came and ruined the picture.
Our bodies were made not for the grave. Christ died; He arose and lives forever.

The body, just like humanity, has frailties from the top to bottom.
The body, whether young or old—the plastic surgeon will fix the problem.
It really is getting out of control, people wanting to look young and only ten.
The best-kept secret in staying young is reading the Bible from start to end.
The mind, soul, and body are at their best when humbled and on bended knee.
God wants you to know He's always in control from sea to shining sea.

Our bodies were made to last forever; then sin came and ruined the picture.
Our bodies were made not for the grave. Christ died; He arose and lives forever.

C+RAD

PoetryIOI 2H

It takes a desire to apply courtesy and kindness
To a world that evolves in sheer chaos and blindness.
Every world leader needs to drop the "talk to the hand" phrase.
So please listen to one another without any propaganda clichés.

What will it take to show kindness all around?
Start helping and caring, then watch the turnaround.
All it takes is simplicity and a very willing heart
Make amends toward each other, then begin a new start.

Agree to disagree on priorities and stop all the hassle.
Don't become a miser in your twenty-first-century post castle.
Do for others that you would have others do for you—
One of many golden rules Christ would want us to do.

What do you think makes the world go around?
Then again, what do you want not ever to be found?
Questions like these should bring us all to our knees.
Let Christ's love be applied toward all, if you will please.

C+RAD

Poetry101 21

We're all from different upbringings and surroundings.
We're all plagued by Facebook and overcrowding.
Day by day, we drive, walk, or run by each other,
Going about our lives, lacking a little of life's luster.
Its only human; we're too busy just to stop and take notice
In a rapid pace world of technology, and still yet no focus.

Humans—yes, that's what we all are.
Humans—we tend to be a little bizarre.

Face it, we're all different yet come from one mold.
Face it, God gave us His Son, Jesus, to behold.
Still we go about life in ignorance toward each other
Until a fork in our life catches our heart to discover
A loved one, a friend, or even who—me? Ourselves
Have received bad news that hits home and compels.

Humans—yes, that's what we all are.
Humans—we tend to be a little bizarre.

Whether young or old, humans need each other.
Whether young or old, with God you're my brother.
What God can do for us all willingly, it is no secret.
He'll surprise us unexpectedly when we least expect it.
He pardons all with His arms stretched wide open.
His amazing love and forgiveness are truly pure golden.

Humans—yes, that's what we all are.
Humans—we tend to be a little bizarre.

C+RAD

PoetrylOl 2j

Growing old to the believer is the way to the fountain of youth.
Christ came into your heart, showing you His wonderful truth
It's a done deal though yet we age; still we're young in His Spirit.
His forgiveness is unsurpassed—something we should never forget.

Joy and gladness are in the heart of every believer.
Sadness and gloom fill the heart of every unbeliever.
Take note of this: rain falls on the good and the bad.
Even one better, we're adopted; guess what—He's our dad.

Yes, at times troubles and worries suck the joy of life's luster.
Just remember it's by His strength only and not ours to muster.
A very good frame of mind is built by reading of His Word.
Be ready for life; it will test you on all that you have heard.

So go ahead and ask yourself, do you truly feel young at heart?
Just know He willingly took your place, from the very start.
Remember He paid a tremendous debt—a debt that we all owed
When God saw the love on the cross that His dear Son showed.

C+RAD

Poetry101 2K

Because of sin, this world continues to lament and travail.
Because of sin, God's wrath plummets and impales.
Disobedience brings consequences—some big, some small—
On a world spiraling downward, kicking and ranting overall.
Noah, a man well favored and obedient with a godly heart,
Obeyed the voice of God to build a boat He called the ark.

Before Christ's return, the weather and environment will assail.
Before Christ's return, judgment on this world will prevail.

Judgment was pronounced since the coming of sin.
Judgment uppercut the Devil right smack in his chin.
The king of doubt and despair made a plan for man to fear.
This plan caused man to err, to fall from grace and swear.
One thing to never, ever do is challenge God; this is very true.
God wants everyone to repent and change to a life that's oh, so new.

Before Christ's return, the weather and environment will assail.
Before Christ's return, judgment on this world will prevail.

The light of every believer is coming back very soon.
The light of every believer—Jesus with His radical platoon.
The hope of every believer is the cross and empty tomb.
The cry of any unbeliever will always be doom and gloom.
God is the God of second chances toward a repented heart,
Wanting all to understand that He loved us from the very start.

Before Christ's return, the weather and environment will assail.
Before Christ's return, judgment on this world will prevail.

C+RAD

Poetry101 2L

The joy of every believer is knowing you've been redeemed.
The Enemy second-guessed his plan, only to be babbled and then reamed.
We're kind of like superheroes when called to listen, pray, or encourage
When led by the Father's Spirit in a world filled with no purpose.

Remember, we're soldiers of the faith and not of this filthy flesh.
Jesus, the Son of God, our example, took time to pray and refresh.
It is so encouraging with all liberty to fully praise and worship,
To feed upon His Word together, leading to a better fellowship.

If need be, challenge yourself if you're stuck in a faith routine basis.
Have a character like Uriah on guard in your God-given vocations.
With God, learn to listen, wait, and be patient; then stand still.
His Word moves forward, never backward; He does all to fulfill.

Yet while we live and breathe in this, our fleshly tent,
Be ready always, listening for the trumpets call the ascent.
Time waits for the Lord in all things; this for sure is true.
We prepare ourselves down here as He prepares up there anew.

C+RAD

Poetry101 2M

Life is precious in the eyes of a loving God, this for you and me.
Life is precious; His only Son died so the world would be free.
We all adore life when a new baby has been born.
Yet this sinful world will take the life of any unborn.
This mixed-up world has its agenda, saving mammals rather than humans.
The idiotic light was on when sin entered, twisting the mind with confusions.

Life is the blood that Jesus shed upon a wooden tree.
Life has a purpose for all that Jesus wants everyone to see.

The Enemy of our soul wants only full control.
The Enemy is limited; this God wants you to know.
The Devil is against every believer standing for the King of Kings.
He will do everything to curtail, yet eternal love stands far in between,
Lest we forget the power of the shed blood of Jesus, the eternal Lamb,
Stained on the doorpost of every believer's heart praising Jesus—He's the man.

Life is the blood that Jesus shed upon a wooden tree.
Life has a purpose for all that Jesus wants everyone to see.

Don't take life for granted; live it while on God's plan.
Don't let the Devil steal your soul; He'll try if he can.
The Devil will try a believer until the Word tells him to flee.
An unrepentant unbeliever—"It's only party time!"—is sad to see.
Taking one's own life whether a believer or unbeliever stands with God—
This separates the finite and infinite, where one goes from here and beyond

Life is the blood that Jesus shed upon a wooden tree.
Life has a purpose for all that Jesus wants everyone to see.

C+RAD

Poetry101 2N

When sunlight strikes falling raindrops in the air,
They act like prisms that form a rainbow oh, so fair,
A division of white light into many beautiful colors,
Forming a long, roundarch high above with wonders.

Legend recalls a boiling pot of gold at one end.
People look, hoping to find something to spend.
Anyone looking for something way beyond your reach,
The rainbow admiration only will try to make you a leech.

But don't give up now; I'm no leprechaun, you see.
Jump up, click your heels, and then count to three.
Believing in something is just only the beginning.
Bear in mind it's worth the wait and all your persisting.

Don't start giving up on life and all its ups and downs,
Feeling like you're in a circus or maybe one of the clowns.
God has a purpose for everyone; you need to wait and see.
That pot of gold way over the rainbow waits for you and me.

C+RAD

PoetryIOI 20

How many blessings can you count without any doubt on one hand?
How many blessings? It takes only one to make you feel quite grand.
God just knows how to reward and bless believers all around.
He'll even make you giddy like a big kid acting like a clown.
He knows there are times that will be hard and also questionable,
Even when prayers seem to be heavy and not very penetrable.

God is a God that surely loves constant and persistent prayer.
God takes care of all matters, is all-knowing, and is fully aware.

We need to be very steadfast and ready to hear His voice.
We need to be in the Word and be reminded of the Enemy's ploys.
The Word directs us toward being ready like an athlete or soldier.
David proved this while shepherding sheep; God made him bolder.
The Word is powerful and enabling toward a willing heart
To bring a change to unbelievers—a fresh and brand-new start.

God is a God that surely loves constant and persistent prayer.
God takes care of all matters, is all—knowing, and is fully aware.

Remember, your name is written in His book He holds so dear.
Remember our Enemy, chained and bound, for one thousand years.
Yes, from the very beginning, and for sure all the way to the end,
Jesus, the Son of God, always lights your path through thick or thin
Like a boat being tossed round about in gale or rough stormy seas.
Jesus is waiting to transform hearts that are willing to be set free.

God is a God that surely loves constant and persistent prayer.
God takes care of all matters, is all knowing, and is fully aware.

C+RAD

Poetry101 2P

Wow, just after the Thanksgiving Day feast, it's the real turkeys that come out,
The Black Friday shopping sprees clogging freeways and store aisles throughout,
People running and pushing their way through for the ultimate deal in the store,
Only to watch themselves on the late news at eleven, surviving the holiday war.

We as humans take on the mentality of mad cows through every holiday year
As the world strategically plans out future profit shares for the upcoming marketer.
On every holiday it seems to be upon the consumer to give
When every store franchise tantalizes, hoping we're corroborative.

This world has an agenda, which is to satisfy while only to pacify
A populace of people's thinking process on having or wanting to overbuy.
Crazy as this may seem, it works; just look inside your packed garage.
Storing small and big items other than autos was the true main cause.

The Bible directs us to be wise stewards in all our giving and buying.
Helping someone less fortunate when able is quite gratifying.
Father God gave His only Son to die for and redeem a crooked world.
Let us remember this Thanksgiving Day Christ's love He gave, and herald.

C+RAD

PoetryIOI 2Q

The Hawaiian Islands—each one a stepping stone toward sheer tropical paradise.
The Hawaiian Islands—known for kicking back; there's no time to rush otherwise.
Each island is truly beautiful, yet different in so many ways.
Which brings to mind that the goddess Pele, like a woman, will set you ablaze.
Just all-around captivating is each island with its panoramic scenery
As trade-wind breezes bring some tropical rain, dampening all lovely greenery.

Each island is just as gratifying and gorgeous as the next,
Each having a character of folklore so suspiciously downright vexed.

Plenty of time to just relax and renew your body and spirit.
Plenty of time to enjoy some sun and darken to a tropical tan pigment.
Clear, vibrant turquoise beaches that mirrors the sky naturally you'll agree.
Black or white sun-bleached sand, a true joy and a must to see.
The culture and lifestyle of any Hawaiian is seasoned with family love.
This love is passed on from generation to generation, coming from Jesus above.

Each island is just as gratifying and gorgeous as the next,
Each having a character of folklore so suspiciously downright vexed.

There is never enough time to see the sites on a one- or two-week visit.
There is always time to change your mind and the tickets at the very last minute.
Just make one visit to any of the islands; you'll never want to leave.
The Bible gives us a little taste of heaven to all who will believe.
This world and other worlds unknown are just a fingerprint or type,
This from God the true Creator and His Son, Jesus—every believer's delight.

Each island is just as gratifying and gorgeous as the next.
Each having a character of folklore so suspiciously downright vexed.

C+RAD

Poetry101 2R

Are you a good or bad person? Just which one would you say?
If a bad person, let's just see what the Bible reads, okay?
Psalm one describes a bad person as ungodly and one who will perish;
Not starting or sounding good so far—something I hope you won't relish.

Psalm fourteen describes a bad person or fool saying God doesn't exist.
A man named Cain became a fool, gave God attitude while shaking his fist.
So the road for a bad person, I hope, isn't your cup of tea.
Jesus came to save both bad and good people, to liberate and set free.

Now don't get me wrong; you can be good and yet not make the grade.
Being good doesn't quite make it if you're playing a silly game of charades.
It's just half of the puzzle, and Jesus wants the other half complete.
God knows the character of a willing heart, making it as strong as concrete.

God knows His creation better than they themselves; this is so very true.
He has endless never-ending patience while waiting with love for you.
The Word of God is full of promises for the good and contrite heart.
This is to all who have a willing heart and want a brand-new start.

C+RAD

PoetryIOI 2§

The house of the Lord is a place of refuge and a haven for imperfect people
The house of the Lord is a place of expectancy and assurance, all under a steeple.
This world is for sure the opposite of all what God has for you and I;
He wants us to know there's a place we can go to pour out our heart and cry.
In the beginning you may ask yourself, "Hey, is this place for me?"
Yet all along in your struggle to be strong, we find that He holds the key.

God welcomes all who have appetites for the truth and desire His understandings.
God welcomes all who are weighed down with problems and misunderstandings.

The house of the Lord is a house of prayer for the mind, soul, and spirit.
The house of the Lord we gather in for His Word to listen to and be adherent.
The Good Shepherd Jesus likens us all to a feeble animal known as a sheep.
He called His disciples to pray with Him, yet only to find them asleep.
The Enemy, the Devil, wants you to think he has control of all your faculties.
He also wants you to continue to blame God for all the world's catastrophes.

God welcomes all who have appetites for the truth and desire His understandings.
God welcomes all who are weighed down with problems and misunderstandings.

Singing and rejoicing are what we'll do when we're all in heaven,
Singing and rejoicing to Jesus, our King, in one huge thunderous session.
We all like yelling, ranting, and raving for our favorite sport or team;
Then come Sunday or any church day, we barely have strength or self-esteem.
God has love for you and knows all the struggles we go through.
King David wrote psalms of praise, singing away his problems—"Adieu."

God welcomes all who have appetites for the truth and desire His understandings.
God welcomes all who are weighed down with problems and misunderstandings.

C+RAD

Poetry101 2T

God knows the heart of every believer, whether happy, sad, or true.
It is written in a book called the Bible to guide and help us through.
He extends His hand to a world that kicks and shuns His love every time.
His brow, side, hands, and feet are marked with depths of love for you and I.

The Bible cries out to unbelievers needing to turn from their way.
It saddens His heart seeing unbelievers not willing to listen and obey.
The Bible nudges, reminding believers to keep their heart and mind focused.
Jesus prayed for Peter and for us because the Devil is out looking to blame us.

Love is the key keeping us on our knee in fighting any spiritual battle.
Michael and Gabriel, the true Twin Towers—watch out; they know how to grapple.
The believer's weapons are spiritual, not earthly, to withstand all Enemy ploys.
God gives His children spiritual discernment to know all the Enemy's decoys.

Becoming a believer takes a willing desire that can only come from God.
He knows your heart; He is the Creator to those who say yes with a nod.
His love is so true in becoming brand-new, making you happy when you're sad.
Now your name is written in His book He holds with love; you'll be very glad.

C+RAD

Poetry1O1 2U

The Christmas story was foretold with man's disobedience in the book of Genesis.
The Christmas story is a story of love, Father God sending His only Son to save us.
God's plan is steadfast and true; the character we chose turned to be untrue.
Yet Jesus, the Rock of all ages, came to save man from darkness and sin's sinew.
The Devil, laughing and snickering, was held limited in the face of a knowing God,
Thinking that he had a checkmate move while putting on a slithery façade.

Emmanuel, God with us—a name all believers should not forget.
Emmanuel, synonymous with love, making unbelievers repent.

There was no room found at the inn for Joseph and Mary that day to stay.
There was no room in this world, yet love from above came down and made a way.
Our mind and heart tend to be overcrowded with a bunch of meaningless things.
But the Christmas story reminds us of all the many blessings that He brings.
That night shepherds kept watch as hosts of angels proclaimed His star so bright.
"Away in a Manger," "We Three Kings," and "Silent Night," they lilted with delight.

Emmanuel, God with us—a name all believers should not forget.
Emmanuel, synonymous with love, making unbelievers repent.

If ever a story that is very true brought lots of joy with so many tears,
If ever a story helped both believers and nonbelievers to a godly fear,
Christmas joy came wrapped in swaddling clothes, perfectly and so innocently.
To an almost completely darkened world, oh, His love was ready unconditionally.
What is your story all about that you may or may not want to share?
One thing I do know—He's ready to listen to all happy or sad hearts with prayer.

Emmanuel, God with us—a name all believers should not forget.
Emmanuel, synonymous with love, making unbelievers repent.

C+RAD

Poetry101 2V

Isn't life swell when everyone's your pal? Yet still there's something that's missing.
Life is tough when your armor's all off and you're dealing with some misgivings.
So don't short yourself; God has the right stuff in His Word and also through prayer.
Send up a flare in the form of a prayer while waiting patiently; He's fully aware.

24-7, here and in heaven, He knows all your dire requests.
God will show He's no Curly, Larry, or Moe yet always knows what's best.
In the race called life, it's not for the swift, but for all that will endure to the end.
Trust in His Son; He and the father are one and comforting again and again.

In all your tasks it won't add up like math; be on guard while reading His Word.
Sure it's crazy when things find a way to make you irritable, miserable, or absurd.
This too remember—we're just passing through, as He said, and not of this world.
He sent His Son to get the job done of saving a world He created and affirmed

Now isn't life swell when Jesus is your pal? He'll be with you till the very end.
His love and grace will take us to a place that is more than just a haven.
It's almost the hour, and time winding down, the Devil now on reserved power.
He knows he'll be going down to a place called hell, reserved for him forever.

C+RAD

Poetry101 2W

Every new year, God waits patiently on a world He created and holds very dear.
Every new year, God waits, for time shall be at hand for this His Son to appear.
We are directed to comfort one another while waiting for His glorious return.
We don't know the day or hour yet wait expectantly for each day to adjourn.
God is the author of time; time follows Him, and no one or thing can change this.
Not a prophet, apostle, disciple or any one willingly luring with a deceptive kiss.

God only knows when His Son shall appear, taking back a world so lost in despair
God shall open the eyes of Israel to bring healing, revealing things still unclear.

God's own love poured out on the just, while judgment on all who received a mark.
God's own love wipes away all tears, sending the Devil to a place he'll embark.
Heaven awaits all believers that have accepted Jesus as their Lord and Savior.
Hell awaits those that chose the mark, putting their trust in a deceiving faker.
Time will be no more, just sanctified saints giving praise to Jesus everyday.
When we are in heaven, no more Monopoly, passing go, or even utility taxes to pay.

God only knows when His Son shall appear, taking back a world so lost in despair.
God shall open the eyes of Israel to bring healing, revealing things still unclear.

Start out this new year right and turn your heart over to the Redeemer.
Start out this new year right; it must come from your heart to be a believer.
Jesus is the door to everyone's heart; He'll knock till you willingly open your heart.
Come just as you are, like a sheep out from pasture, all dirty, tattered, and scarred.
Jesus, known as the spotless Lamb, given as a ransom for oh, so many
At the Father's request, happily gave His life for a world that wasn't ready.

God only knows when His Son shall appear, taking back a world so lost in despair.
God shall open the eyes of Israel to bring healing, revealing things still unclear.

C+RAD

Poetry101 2X

This world justifies remedial insight through Greek, human, or plain stupid thinking.
Never add or take from the Bible, or somebody will have to do much explaining.
People, when questioned on what they believe, first state they are a good person.
The Bible says there is no one good but God alone; gives clarity and justification.

The world has a lot of input but zero quality output, which stands to all reasoning.
Today's technology in hand morbidly controls minds to relative thinking.
We are creatures of habit, still choosing things that are bad rather than good.
His sheep know and listen for His voice while directed toward a better livelihood.

The Bible was written by inspired men and explains how life should be simple.
The philosophy this world gave is heartburn, and your mind is completing a circle.
This world still believes we have primitive cousins that are a barrel of laughs.
Proof is in the pudding; our country is run by primitive Republicans and Democrats.

Who are you identifying with, the Creator or primitive cousin?
Is your thinking relatively dependent, or absolutely pure with no gumption?
Then turn to the basic instruction before leaving earth—the Bible, for all it's worth.
Believe me, you can have your cake, eat it too, and of course many other desserts.

C+RAD

PoetryIOI 2y

This country will ring in the new year for the 238th time.
This country with economic, health, and foreign issues, dropping to a moral decline.
Proverbs one: God laughs at anyone who disregards and disdains His counsel.
He knows our government and all lobbyists are nothin' but dirty rotten scoundrels.
Yet every four years, there's always a change or staying the course that will take place
For all the rich and people with monies that this country is told to embrace.

When a country is not truly represented for all people, starting from the top;
When a country presents a dogmatic approach, twisting truth soon better stop

We all want the new year everywhere to start rightly, not two steps backward.
We all would like both federal and state to return half of what we all filed for.
Joseph was made governor in all of Egypt for his godly wisdom and discernment.
Pharaoh, witnessing the Spirit of God in Joseph, made him to bow in reverence.
The eyes of world leaders are blinded by greed, power, and all the Devil will control.
This divides all countries and nations, forsaking godly fear, not willing to be whole.

When a country is not truly represented for all people, starting from the top;
When a country presents a dogmatic approach, twisting truth soon better stop.

Desiring to run for any public office should never be done for financial status.
Desire to run for what a country needs; God is waiting and willing to guide us.
Remember, this world will do the opposite of what God would have as established,
Keeping every agenda hidden so meticulously, then at the end only to be shafted.
God called a man named Jonah to go preach to the hearts waiting at Nineveh.
Nineveh heard the message and then repented; pray we do the same, oh yeah!

When a country is not truly represented for all people, starting from the top;
When a country presents a dogmatic approach, twisting truth soon better stop.

C+RAD

PoetryI0I 2Z

The sky and heaven are the limits in a world full of technology.
Whether writer or poet you're well versed on the correct terminology.
Dream big and never small, optimizing your gray matter on many goals.
This will help even more when God is aware of all you propose.

Sure, in the beginning it is a vast mountain or a long stretch of a road.
Remember, a two-strand rope is stronger than one, just in case of life's overload.
Stay focused on your goals by prayer, Bible reading, and also church attendance.
In doing this, God will carry you and reassure you through all your assessments.

Please remember it's a day-by-day journey. Don't rush this, yet endure with faith,
Seasoned in the difficult times when your weakness is strengthened by His grace.
As crazy as this may seem, it's amazing how He orchestrates behind the scene.
He'll give you supernatural strength like Sampson's in defeating many Philistines.

Be all that you're willing to be, and never give up or sell yourself short.
Keep yourself in check by His Word, reminding you Jesus is the Lord.
It is never too late, whether young or old, to dream or have many goals.
He rewards all those who seek His Word, which comforts and consoles.

C+RAD

PoetryIOI

A Happy Person Whose God Is the Lord

Happy is a person whose God is the Lord—
The Lord God Almighty, one who is adored,
The Ancient of Days, and the song in the night.
Night obeys His presence, for He is the light.
The fowler or fool sidesteps His presence,
His presence so majestic with purity and radiance,
Radiance with eternal love and unending forgiveness.

C+RAD

Poetry101

The Fool Still Says

The fool still says that God doesn't exist,
For a fool's heart isn't ready to commit
To something he thinks he'll regret.
When it's too late, his soul is in hell instead.
When Christ died for all and took our debt,
He freely took and gave us His very best—
The best that God's only Son gave us for His eternal rest.

C+RAD

Poetry101

The Fruits for Our Joy

The fruits of the Spirit are for every believer's joy,
The joy He gives to us when evil wants to annoy,
Annoy when evil strikes our attention like a decoy,
A decoy that's only deployed and not some real McCoy.
The Enemy, the Devil, will try everything to ruffle us,
All who willingly put their faith in the Lord Jesus.
The Lord Jesus helps all our bereavements.

C+RAD

Poetry101

Blessed Is the Man Whose God Is the I AM

Blessed is the man whose God is The I AM,
The I AM who was and is our sacrificial Lamb
The Lamb of God eternal, who truly gives a ram,
The ram Abraham gave, foreshadowing God's heavenly plan,
A plan to save the first Adam, who became a sinful man,
A sinful man God's Son bore to eclipse the Devil's scam.
The Devil is now eating his peanut butter and jam.

C+RAD

Poetry101

Nations Rage Over Vain Things

Why do nations rage in a world, plotting vain things,

Vain things which are run by obnoxious evil kings,

Earthly kings needing remembrance of who's the King of Kings.

The King of Kings is Jesus with the salvation He brings,

Bringing this to a world caught up in ungodly things,

Things distracting coming from the Devil; his evil he'll fling,

Only to be de-stinged and de-winged by Jesus, every believer's King.

C+RAD

Poetry101

Troubles and Vices Against Me

Lord, how the world has and will trouble me.
Very many have taken their vices against me.
Many will say troubling things about me.
Yet, O Lord, you are my shield and buckler for me.
I cried to you, Lord; in my strength you heard me.
When I turn in each day, then you awake and bless me.
You strengthen me more than who are against me.
Arise, O lord, and conquer my enemies for me.

C+RAD

Poetry101

O God of My Righteousness

Hear me when I call, O God of my righteousness.
My righteousness is because of your Son, who is the Lord Jesus,
Jesus who gives to all who ask for His steadfastness,
His steadfastness in a world full of much sadness,
Sadness He'll change toward His morning gladness.
His gladness He'll give to hearts becoming so anxious,
Anxious yet awaiting to ascend up to heavenly mansions.

C+RAD

Poetry101

Path of the Wicked

Do not enter the path of the wicked,
The wicked who at all times are rotten bigots,
Bigots who have a false appearance,
An appearance that can be truly vicious,
So vicious their character is downright religious,
So religious with a heart without any forgiveness,
Forgiveness from God's beloved Son, the Lord Jesus.

C+RAD

Poetry101

Wisdom and Understanding

Get wisdom, Get understanding,
Understanding that can be so heavenly enchanting,
Enchanting without any major borderline calamity,
Calamity that comes from a world so discouraging,
Discouraging when potential young minds becoming less determining.
Determining comes from searching many hearts worth purchasing,
which God has dealt with us through His Son's forgivings.

C+RAD

Fear the Lord

Fear the Lord and depart from evil,
The evil that continues to creep upon many people.
People are becoming very lethargic and feeble.
Feebleness can weaken a mind becoming deceitful,
Deceitful when evil overrules good, loving people,
People seeing false leadership, becoming predictable imbeciles,
Imbeciles running a nation—which is very unthinkable.

C+RAD

Poetry101

He Corrects in Love

For whom the Lord loves, He corrects,
Correcting those who confess with sorrowful laments,
Laments from events the Lord knows and comprehends,
Comprehends our sin nature can be truly intense,
Intense by wrong friends with worldly attitudes they posses.
Possess your own soul when you share the truth with assurance,
knowing Christ is every believer's reassurance.

C+RAD

Poetry101

Hate Evil

The fear of the Lord is to hate evil.
Evil, like a weasel, knows not what is needful—
Needful and heedful to His truths that are peaceful,
Peaceful for a world caught up in such upheaval,
Upheaval growing rapidly when good is bad and illegal,
Illegal when our rights and freedoms are taken away from the people.
People we all are, and in need of a God-fearing revival.

C+RAD

Poetry101 3A

What is your status quo in this life, rich in heart or heart in riches?
What is your status quo, a man after God's heart or a man who is religious?
Since the disobedience of man that brought on shame and degradation,
Promoting a puffed up attitude without a means for any liberation,
A young man by the name of David, a shepherd of sheep for his father, Jesse,
Spent time meditating in the field, awaiting God's love, which was very plenty.

The heart of a person defines one and reveals their true character
The heart of a person God wants to change from a sinful to unsinful nature.

Lest we forget that it is a choice—a choice that He wants us to make—
Lest we forget His Son Jesus chose the way of the cross for all eternity to take,
As human beings we're inadequate in choices we're rushed to make.
We also tend to go with feelings, not weighing the facts, which ends up in a mistake,
Presenting a lot of literal jargon that this world confuses in all simple minds.
It's no wonder nothing is done in a free country when out to lunch all the time.

The heart of a person defines one and reveals their true character.
The heart of a person God wants to change from a sinful to unsinful nature.

So be sure on your status in life and upon where you'll spend all eternity.
Don't worry; it is upon Christ's shed blood that redeems both you and me.
You can take it to the bank that God hasn't left us; it's we who left Him.
A country founded on godly principles, and now our eyes growing very dim.
The outcomes for all who put their faith in Jesus have nothin' about which to worry
For the rest of those that still haven't, for all eternity will they truly be sorry.

The heart of a person defines one and reveals their true character.
The heart of a person God wants to change from a sinful to unsinful nature.

C+RAD

PoetryIOI 3B

The day the earth stands still will be the day all believers are taken up and away,
Leaving earth with no problems, just solemn woes for those who have to stay.
God is a just and patient Creator; it's just that all are in need of a redeeming Savior.
He sent His Son to redeem a world He created, caught in unheavenly behavior.

His Son lives a sinless life; only God the Father directs Him in all on what to do.
The same with believers, though not sinless; it's our life that He helps us through.
A man named Abraham God the Father directed because he first believed.
Promising and making a covenant, he became a father of many through his seed.

This world quakes, knowing hell will come out whether dawn or midnight break.
Vast world governments will globalize regarding what is truly at stake.
All hearts all around will tremble in fear, yet a facade of a leader will soon appear.
This facade of a leader will tantalize with lies and, just for a while, remove all fear.

In the very beginning, God has been in control; He wants you to see.
Whether it is fourth down and long or two seconds to go and down by a three,
His eyes are always on His beloved, watching as each day rolls on by.
You'll find comfort that's always found in His Word, and love for you and I.

C+RAD

Poetry101 3C

Immoral popular people of the world dress up as advertising billboards for show.
Immoral popular people just stymie young and immature minds who dunno.
In thinking on starting a culture revolution to behave in a way for attention,
They've watched too many *Twilight Zone* marathons, or they're from another dimension.
Immoral behavior spoils the hearts and minds, leading toward disarray.
Immoral people have too much time on hand to behave in a way that feels okay.

An idle mind is the Devil's playground for crooked and misguided behavior.
An idle mind can only be changed by a caregiving redeeming Savior.

"The Devil made me do it" was and still is the crutch word play of the day.
"The Devil made me do it"—a choice that cripples the mind wanting to disobey.
It goes without saying, you reap what you sow or you sow what you reap.
Whom do you identify with, a meddling troubled goat or a dumb humble sheep?
If a lot of pride is dwelling in your life, then you're butting in the wrong direction.
The Bible will answer all your questions and also show you your true reflection.

An idle mind is the Devil's playground for crooked and misguided behavior.
An idle mind can only be changed by a caregiving redeeming Savior.

Let's face it, some people are not able to distinguish between true reality and fake.
Let's face it, people are putting their souls on the line not knowing what's at stake.
People going about life ignorantly, living their life without any moral obligation.
God sent His Son, Jesus, to take our place and debt for His great salvation.
Believe me, there are people holding desperately to their own initial fate,
Only to miss out on Jesus in their life and forever be eternally separate.

An idle mind is the Devil's playground for crooked and misguided behavior.
An idle mind can only be changed by a caregiving redeeming Savior.

C+RAD

Poetry101 3D

This world is getting darker and separating itself from the true light of the Son,
Always in a mindset state, soon globalizing, becoming a worldly nation as one.
Greed, pride, and hatred—the three derelicts from their evil father of pride—
Will do everything and anything to cloud the minds of people already stupefied.

Remember, we're just a marred lump of clay, and the Creator is the loving potter.
He lovingly waits with His arms wide open to change all improper hearts to proper.
Yet the Enemy, the Devil, is out, and in force, knowing his time is now at hand.
Jesus, the Son of God, at the Fathers command will be ready to highly reprimand.

Though this world will not budge or change until toward the very end,
When God calls the loving departed first while snatching all believers to ascend,
This will be the wildest and most chaotic period the world will ever see—
A world finally without God and the Holy Spirit, not restraining, with no apology.

The time is now at hand for all believers to go and take their stand.
The unbelievers need to wake up or forever be judged and damned.
God is and shall always be; He has no pleasure in the death of the wicked.
If they will just turn from their evil ways, He'll have their sinful hearts omitted.

C+RAD

Poetry101 3E

Rain is a necessity for the replenishing and washing of the environment,
just as the Spirit of God soothes the soul and washes away the violent.
In a rapid-paced world where time is short and there is not much financial gain,
Weather all around changes as areas that were green are now dry without rain.
Climate change and greenhouse gases are melting away the huge arctic polar caps.
Many world governments are letting out the cats, only to be ruined by hungry fat rats.

God made the world so fresh and clean; man gave into sin, doing 180 degrees.
God made man to care for Eden, and man yielded to sin; he became lost, not free.

We're people of habit; when we're to do right, we end up doing the wrong.
We're people needing His help daily to become spiritually, not physically, strong.
Paul the apostle wrote that people will do the wrong before ever doing the right.
Paul explains it is not on our strength to muster, but on the Holy Spirit's might.
God wants all to see that man became lost when he disobeyed His solemn instruction.
He listened to the wrong voice; his soul and mind were headed for destruction.

God made the world so fresh and clean; man gave into sin, doing 180 degrees.
God made man to care for Eden, and man yielded to sin; he became lost, not free.

What is more devastating, a world without water or a world without God?
What is so asinine is all world governments fighting to see who's the top dog.
Pride ruins a nation and the people that are caught struggling in its web.
This is what happens when you invite the living dead into your own cozy bed.
God will send His Son soon to bring home His lovely bride, the church,
Out from a world lost and darkened that will soon take upon His scourge.

God made the world so fresh and clean; man gave into sin doing 180 degrees.
God made man to care for Eden, and then man yielded to sin; he became lost, not free.

C+RAD

Poetry101 3F

As day turns to night and night turns to day,
This world that we live in is still in much disarray.
Overpopulation, immorality, and the world's economy are on the decline.
Crooked people and government lobbyists are ruining a world only to undermine.

Off-ramps are a certain sign for deprived people looking for a handout;
The opposite for crooked-minded people holding government office, selling out.
Diplomacy and democracy have grown wings and soon will fly away
In a world spiraling downward like a mouth full of tooth decay.

All smartphones and smart TV screens surely will tantalize the mind.
People hunger for the newest technology, or else they will whine.
Technology, whether good or bad, is judged by the eye of the beholder.
Forbid it be made in the US; no one wants something that's only mediocre.

It's a shame a world created by a loving God, only to be ruined by ungodly men,
Trusts only in people like themselves who live by the seven deadly sins.
For this reason, immoral and weak minds blame or don't trust in a loving God.
The Devil will take people's minds and hearts, all becoming lost and charmed.

C+RAD

Poetry101 3G

The world, God created; He spoke the Word out, and it came to be.
The world God created as perfect as a picture would bring us all to our knees.
Da Vinci, Van Gogh, or Rembrandt are famous painters the world has known.
Marvel on what God has expressed in the talents that they have shown.
Would you give one million dollars for something that's old and not of value?
Mankind gave up on paradise for stinkin' worldly problems; it's sad but true.

God is the Creator of everything no matter how minute or universal.
God is the Creator of everything, yet still His presence is controversial.

God is and will always be unmatched by far, while little man can only tinker.
God is and will always be patient with man, no matter how much he's a stinker.
Greatness can only be achieved by true wisdom that comes from above—
His vast presence far above the heavens and His love that swoons like a dove.
There's just no comparison in what man tries to whittle away in striving for his greatness.
While here in a tent, still ever aging, he'll be as rambunctious and outrageous

God is the Creator of everything, no matter how minute or universal.
God is the Creator of everything, yet still His presence is controversial.

Just imagine looking through the eyes of God, how caring He really is,
Knowing He sent His Son, Jesus, bringing hope to a world He'll forgive.
His eyes are ever watching His creation, then how much more of thee.
Day upon day, night upon night, God never sleeps, yet humbles us to our knee.
God is always on alert to fight our battles, as He did in helping out Daniel.
Daniel was in prayer for a long duration; God sent an angel named Gabriel.

God is the Creator of everything, no matter how minute or universal.
God is the Creator of everything, yet still His presence is controversial.

C+RAD

Poetry101 3H

The night skies are so secret and very quiet while being cloaked all around,
With just the lights of the stars that twinkle and the moonbeams that shine down.
People venture out, gazing whether by walking, by running, or even by car.
Some even wait for the perfect moment to make a wish on seeing a falling star.

Moonlit skies envelop one's heart when next to the one you love,
Bringing home to your heart just how much of God's love is from above.
Just imagine heaven—all the heavenly host longing and wanting to see
People being humble under a church steeple, praising Jesus, and all on one knee.

Darkness all around just for a moment, till the great light of heaven is shone.
Worldly people doing harm in the dark think God won't see what He condones.
When God speaks the Word, darkness has too flee, always obeying His command—
Something the Devil will never agree on, though he thinks he has the upper hand.

There's nothing wrong in enjoying a gorgeous, beautiful moonlight sky
When your heart and mind are tired and wanting to just let out such a sigh.
His creation is not only beautiful during the demanding daylight hours;
It's also enjoyed by the two-legged or four-legged beastie growlers and howlers.

C+RAD

Poetry101 3i

The wind, so boisterous and powerful whether from the north, south, east, or west;
The wind—no one knows whence it comes or where it goes, but only has a guess.
A man of the Pharisees named Nicodemus, a certain ruler of the Jews
Came to Jesus by night, having many questions in his heart, seeking what to do.
Jesus explained, "You're a teacher of Israel and you know not of these things.
You must be born again of water and the Spirit; this is what the Holy Spirit brings.

The wind, just like any problem, will come out surprisingly from nowhere.
The wind, no matter how strong or weak, will mess up your salon-groomed hair.

Wind is also compared or expressed in referencing the Holy Spirit of God.
Wind, like the Holy Spirit, will blast away a dirty, filthy facade.
Jesus sent the Holy Spirit as a witness and helper for every believer.
He'll continue reminding the world and believers of any foreseen misdemeanors.
The Holy Spirit is a representative of the triune Godhead—Father, Son, and Spirit—
Keeping the world from getting out of hand, that all believers may stay adherent.

The wind, just like any problem, will come out surprisingly from nowhere.
The wind, no matter how strong or weak, will mess up your salon-groomed hair.

Don't let characters of the world stroll into your well-kept arrangements,
Bringing others more devious upon you, scattering and making disarrangements.
Whether you're a good person of the world or a faithful believer in Jesus,
He's the real reason for coming to a world so lost and strewn into many pieces.
There is no one that is good but God only, Jesus told a self-righteous person.
In order to see heaven, you must be born again; this your spiritual conversion.

The wind, just like any problem, will come out surprisingly from nowhere.
The wind, no matter how strong or weak, will mess up your salon-groomed hair.

C+RAD

PoetrylOl 3j

Bike riding is enjoyed by all people, no matter how young or old.
Though when in heaven, we won't ride bikes, but we'll walk on streets of gold.
We ride our bikes everywhere: to the beach, the park, and at off-road sites.
If you're seriously into riding, you wear a uniform that surely fits tight.

Back in the day, if you didn't own a car, a bike was the other alternative,
Yet in a cultural age of technology, riding to work is just a tad bit primitive.
As alternative means are being applied to clear and clean up our environment,
This is true for those who run our government to have a grip on enlightenment

This method of travel is tremendous for the heart, body, and soul of a person.
It benefits everyone to become more fit without weight becoming a burden.
You can become a glutton on most anything you choose to devote yourself for—
A behavior God would have you not struggle in, and one you shouldn't ignore

So make some time to ride a bike and enjoy the freedoms this will bring.
See places and things in a different way; it just may lift your heart to sing.
God has many benefits for all who take the time and enjoy life's scenery.
He wants you to have some outlets in life so you won't become lifeless or dreary.

C+RAD

Poetry101 3K

God, with depths of love, works behind the scenes in people's lives.
God knows the hearts of people and each frail little baby who cries.
We all are very unique in the eyes of a beholding and caring God,
Yet we took on a sinful character so crude, rude, and spitefully odd.
Just a glob of clay in the hands of the Master Sculptor, remolding our imperfections.
Jesus was marred for our imperfections, transforming us toward His affections.

God is omnipotent, omnipresent, and omniscient; also He's the Lamb.
God is just; read Genesis twenty-two—how Abraham with such joy gave a ram.

His Majesty is so grand and untouchable, yet in Jesus He's very attainable.
His thinking is beyond our comprehension yet very remarkably embraceable.
Man's thought process is way out of kilter, needing many thumps on the head.
As old age starts creeping in, his thought process slows to brain farts instead.
God is amazed how we'll justify things without giving any second thought,
Shaking His head as we spilled milk again and broke a jar of applesauce.

God is omnipotent, omnipresent, and omniscient; also He's the Lamb.
God is just; read Genesis twenty-two—how Abraham with such joy gave a ram.

Our frailties as humans will surely make us doubt His Majesty without hesitation.
Our frailties as humans one day will make us exalt an imitator without reservation.
God loves and confides in us no matter how much we dust Him.
He knows about our weaknesses when we're just about to give in.
God is ready when all of mankind will turn their back against Him
The Antichrist, will cause mankind to swoon and then will be condemned.

God is omnipotent, omnipresent, and omniscient; also He's the Lamb.
God is just; read Genesis twenty-two—how Abraham with such joy gave a ram.

C+RAD

Poetry|0| 3L

What would you say is on the heart of a person who's slowly fading away,
Catching a glimpse as they sit or lie while staring in the air with such dismay.
You collect yourself at that point in time, mustering up some reasonable thoughts
As God reminds how wonderfully He made you though sin gave us these flaws.

Your heart, you'll find, leaps for those who are in a mind state of just being.
Being the people who you love and this thought of ever foreseeing.
Death isn't very particular to anyone, whether a believer or unbeliever.
Death to everyone is an unwelcome shadow that will be around sooner or later.

Days turn to weeks, months, and—oh my—already a year.
God is fully aware; it's not ours to ponder on things He truly forbears.
Jesus, son of David, is full of compassion, as David was for almighty God.
David would seek almighty God for advice until He said yes with a nod.

So for a person who fades in and out while time is just passin'by,
The heart and mind are somewhat alert, yet yearning to let out a cry.
God calls His beloved with serenity while still working on the unloved,
Wanting a hope of heaven for those while waiting for their hearts to be adjusted.

C+RAD

Poetry101 3M

The Bible is the Word of God, which gives authority through Jesus, His Son.
The Bible enables believers to go in His authority on all that must be done.
Is authority given to Jesus in heaven and on earth what the Devil stole from man first?
Jesus paid the price in full on the cross—all shame and everything that God cursed.
This authority gives the right for every believer to continue His work and fulfill.
Remember this: only in His authority does He tell you to behold and stand still.

This authority is heavenly, directed with power to go and teach all nations.
This authority is not a hidden or covert operation, but one with love and adoration.

Jesus at twelve years amazed many teachers; He later taught twelve fishermen.
Jesus, ascending to heaven, instructed His disciples to have all men repent from sin.
This authority comes with abundance of grace for the lost and unwanted souls.
Jesus grew in grace with God and man; soon the whole world would see and know.
It takes a desire of the heart and a passion to go teach people of all nations.
You can be young at heart or some old fart; He'll give you heaven's inspiration.

This authority is heavenly directed with power to go and teach all nations.
This authority is not a hidden or covert operation, but one with love and adoration.

Christ has given believers power and authority to go reclaim all for His kingdom.
Christ reminds believers, for His namesake will go through hatred and criticism.
It's *everything* Jesus believed His Father gave Him to bestow on His beloved—
Having a mindful heart in caring and encouraging to all that are being instructed.
Good things are being done; watch out for opposing and criticizing right at your nose.
Yet surely His Word never returns void, transposing to those who willingly chose.

This authority is heavenly, directed with power to go and teach all nations.
This authority is not a hidden or covert operation, but one with love and adoration.

C+RAD

PoetryIOI 3N

Springtime brings a newness of life, a rebirth of many things found on this earth.
Flowers brim with vibrant colors, swaying in meadows for all to observe.
Birds fly above with melodies like larks, enjoying life as they fly by.
Insects or bugs are all the same while bees make honey in ample supply.

Animals are on land while mammals in the ocean enjoy their new pups all around.
Any stray cats or hounds lurking freely are to be caught and placed in a pound
Coming soon: a new world and heaven enjoying a new radiance from the Son.
The old world and heaven soon will be destroyed for what sinful man has done.

The Bible brings glimpses of what will be over on the other side.
Rivers and lakes flow very pristinely, and tasting so sweet that you'll confide.
Early morning air of spring high in the mountains takes your breath away,
The peak looking like a pebble among majestic formations, touching the soul at bay.

Jesus prepares a place in heaven, which springtime is no match for down here.
He lovingly and caring as time ticks close reassures all believers in despair.
So enjoy each day whether in the summer, fall, winter, or spring you hear
With a hope of heaven in your heart the call to ascend up there.

C+RAD

Poetry101 30

What God made and gave, for the benefit of all mankind,
What God cheerfully and without hesitation offered—we declined.
God gave man full rein in Eden on earth, to care for and have dominion.
God gave man a direct command, but man would later slip on his opinion.
Sin has made our bodies very frail, but God—He heals all our wounds.
He sent His Son to a world that was on the verge of becoming very doomed.

The words that were given by the apostles from our Lord Jesus Christ remember
In building yourselves up with holy faith and in the Holy Spirit through prayer.

The Devil and the world speak evil on things that they do not know.
The Devil and the world are like brute beasts corrupting all that they show.
We tend to give the Devil credit for things that God holds him limited on
Especially little things, like gossiping and storytelling directed toward anyone.
The Devil will twist all truth, as he has done from the very beginning.
Give him an inch and he'll take it, knowing that people would rather be sinning.

The words that were given by the apostles from our Lord Jesus Christ remember
In building yourselves up with holy faith and in the Holy Spirit through prayer.

God has given us the choice of what to accept in that which is good or bad.
God gives mankind plenty of time to change and repent from sad to glad.
God knows the heart of man is always thinking and planning evil, almost daily.
The touch of God is the only way to change a stony heart into a little baby.
This can only come to anyone desiring a chance to change their life.
God is always on time, for this will change for good from a life of strife.

The words that were given by the apostles from our Lord Jesus Christ remember
In building yourselves up with holy faith and in the Holy Spirit through prayer.

C+RAD

Poetry101 3P

The alarm on an iPhone wakes you for school, work, or errands
Hit the snooze button just for a minute—oops, get ready for the consequences.
There are times we'll start the day off on the wrong foot, left or right,
Only to realize it's the weekend, stop for a moment, then shout out "All right!"

Each day, things will happen differently regardless if you're a right-hander or left.
Yet every day is a blessing, no matter if the rain falls upon the bad or the blessed.
Your outlook on life depends on your character—yes, this from the inside and out.
Jesus is always curious about your life and heart, if you know what I'm talkin'"bout.

Our mind can get all twisted and torn from weathering all daily life demises,
The same as being able to see life more clearly or else needing better eyeglasses.
Never let a bad day ruin you mentally; let it run like water off a duck's back.
It's easier said than done when putting it into practice and getting the knack.

Remember this: a godly mind humbles while a worldly mind continues to stumble.
His grace and truth are very amiable in helping us through times when disgruntled,
While still here in this fleshly tent and all spent, we're just a-passin' through.
Soon the trumpet sounds the call to ascend while singing and shouting "adieu."

C+RAD

Poetry101 30

Give honor to whom honor is due; this Christ would want us all to do.
Give honor and praise to God, our King; this the nation of Israel misconstrued.
To honor someone in gratitude and go beyond the call of duty or service
Is a blessing that should continue whether at work, school, or in churches
This from God, whom we should always give honor to steadfastly and daily.
Remember, He's a mighty and supreme God, not one to be served shamefacedly.

Give honor to a friend, relative, and also to all Christ-filled believers.
Give honor to people; when doing this, you will build up your faith much deeper.

We all need encouragement in life, especially when situations are beyond our control.
We need a pat on the shoulder to lift our spirits when feeling down in the soul.
Moses encouraged Joshua to lead Israel to a land flowing with milk and honey.
Joshua encouraged Israel to rid the people, for they were getting quite smutty.
God has a way to lift our soul with love full of joy when we're very low.
He takes our hand and leads us tenderly down the straight path that's aglow.

Give honor to a friend, relative, and also to all Christ-filled believers.
Give honor to people; when doing this, you will build up your faith much deeper.

God is more than a friend; He's the Creator of you and me.
God honors all that humble themselves, wanting their hearts to stay free.
God gives praise and honor when a sinner repents from their old ways.
His Word is surely one you'll depend on as angels in heaven give Him praise.
God would love to see humanity set free, in their heart yearning for Him.
He knows it will take a little of His grace; the rest will come from within.

Give honor to a friend, relative, and also to all Christ-filled believers.
Give honor to people; when doing this, you will build up your faith much deeper.

C+RAD

Poetry101 3R

Isn't it a blessing to start the day not having any hiccups?
Enjoying the day, Bible reading and prayer are why there are no mix-ups.
Medicine is for flu symptoms while prayer scatters evil critters away.
Come Wednesday or Sunday Bible studies, you shout "Hip, hip, hooray!"

Just roll with it; you'd be doing the opposite, and you know what I mean.
Before God touched your stinkin' life, you'd holler and shout, makin' a scene.
God uses those natural-born talents you wasted before becoming a believer.
We fail to see He has other plans for us, whether as a preacher or leader.

The heart He is always looking at in everyone, whether thick or thin skin.
The harder the heart or head, the easier for His Word to glance off one's chin.
The love God has for His creation is so infinite no galaxy could ever behold this.
He had love for all twelve of the disciples, even if one would deceive with a kiss.

The world is getting darker faster, and you're color-blind if you don't see this.
The voice of another this world will hear, and it may end up sounding like a hiss.
The sheep know only one voice; Jesus is the voice of the one true Shepherd.
He'll bring His sheep, not goats, to heaven;they gladly repented and surrendered.

C+RAD

Poetry101 3§

This country may have started out with some religious godly principles.
This country, morally defecating, hid behind a religious facade run by imbeciles.
A country run by people who still feel a square peg fits inside a circle,
Liberal news media paid off to hide truth, making the news too controversial
In a land of transaction fees and the home of the less, this will make you wonder
At why we're in a trillion-dollar debt, and at all the monies congress squandered

This country, like others before, will crumble from greed and a demised lifestyle.
This country, like others before, has fallacies in action but declines to reconcile.

Whether God-fearing or ungodly, men are and will always be fallible.
Whether God-fearing or ungodly, all people have a tendency to be gullible
The Lord understands when we lack in studies or prayer becomes an obligation.
Joshua, mistakenly not seeking the Lord, made a covenant with a deceiving nation
Moses was told to speak to the rock, but instead, out of anger, he disobeyed.
This happens when the flesh hinders our being, yet Jesus says "Don't be dismayed."

This country, like others before, will crumble from greed and a demised lifestyle.
This country, like others before, has fallacies in action but declines to reconcile.

Judgments have been declared on this country, condemning a once God-fearing nation.
Judgments have been declared on liberty abuses and a handful of misrepresentation.
When a country chooses to continue wrong with no remorse or sense of guilt,
The spirit of the Antichrist is well at work, harboring until all is fulfilled.
Once again darkness will be upon this earth by choice from ungodly people.
The Holy Spirit is gone and all believers caught up, just before doom's upheaval.

This country, like others before, will crumble from greed and a demised lifestyle.
This country, like others before, has fallacies in action but declines to reconcile.

C+RAD

PoetrylOl 3T

Prayer is a believer's emergency flare or a roadside call signal to God.
The Devil will not have you do this, sending you some misgiving thoughts.
This will change for the better when we start our daily life with a word of prayer.
God is in control, seeing our faith in action, going through some roads of despair.

Life's demises will challenge you, especially when you're a born-again believer.
Yet when we find ourselves in prayer, life will turn out so much sweeter.
We need to glory in trials and weaknesses so that He'll build up our faith.
Jesus spoke this to Paul, which took him to a much higher confident place.

We don't know what tomorrow holds, but we know who holds tomorrow.
God has things lined out; He'll give glad hearts for our sadness and sorrows.
We need to remind ourselves daily that this isn't our home or abode.
Jesus, prepares places for every believer; this His Word tells us to behold.

Strive to pray as the Word says—always—and in this you will not faint.
By this the Devil is limited while his deeds and works are held detained.
This is why—Jesus modeled the example to take the time to pray.
His Father's love drew Him closer, while angels encouraged Him not to sway.

C+RAD

Poetry101 30

The love of and greed for money contaminates all logical reasoning.
The love of and greed for power cheapens a character into weaseling.
Judas, one of the twelve, coveted and was a thief masquerading as a disciple.
He had a heart like the Devil and, betraying innocent blood, became suicidal.
This Devilish desire cheapens a character becoming lifeless and rotten,
Something that we're all aware of, and this activity becomes very common.

The desire for power and fascination with greed date to when the world began.
The desire for power and fascination with greed have corrupted assemblymen.

The Devil will school anyone desiring to become worldly in all matters of life.
The Devil won't hesitate to give you anything, knowing that everyone has a price.
The Devil tempted the Son of God with twisted Scriptures packed with lies.
Jesus answered correctly, having the Devil flee, his tail between his thighs.
The Devil will try you if you're well prepared and dressed, fully equipped.
He's versed in this from tripping many noble and bold people whom he eclipsed.

The desire for power and fascination with greed date to when the world began
The desire for power and fascination with greed have corrupted assemblymen

The eyes of anyone desiring power and greed will blind you from eternal truth.
The eyes of anyone desiring to be free need only to repent from life's untruths.
The first king of Israel, King Saul, had a problem with power going to his head.
Knowing he stood taller than all made him disobey the voice of God instead.
We're no good in the eyes of God, but in Jesus we're redeemed from all untruths.
Jesus gave His life as a ransom for all; this is what God sees as the final proof.

The desire for power and fascination with greed date to when the world began
The desire for power and fascination with greed have corrupted assemblymen.

C+RAD

Poetry101 3V

Attitudes, whether strong or weak—scaling it could lead to some problems
On who started what; be sympathetic, or it could lead to annoying squabbles.
Attitudes turn people's perspectives depending what side of the coin you're on.
It may not be worth dealing with and to say "I just don't give a darn."

Attitudes can be good; they will motivate your personality into healthy thinking,
Like a rock, country, or opera star belting out some real cool professional singing.
Attitudes, whether good or bad, start inside the mind and then travel to the heart.
Having a healthy mind depends on your attitude on how and where you'll start.

Let nothing be done of ambition only, but with an unselfish attitude for others.
Let's look at people's interests first; this opens blessings toward one another.
Let us be humble toward each other, as Christ exemplified this on the cross.
Dying in your own sin—there's no excuse for what will happen at your loss.

The mind God created to be wonderful and resourceful, this all for His glory.
Man then would step in a box he created, leaving God out in such vainglory.
This happens when minds or attitudes are filled with such worries and despair.
This is the reason why Jesus gave His life for sinners; this His Word declares.

C+RAD

Poetry101 3W

Every believer in Christ has a work set apart for His kingdom.
Every believer in Christ should work on their gift God has given in wisdom.
All believers have a gift God bestows on them the day they say, "I repent."
Like snowflakes, differing and unique, this gift is yours, one hundred percent.
This is for you to share in love with all people while building His kingdom,
Reaching many people of color and leading them to Jesus, our true freedom.

Jesus is the chief cornerstone and common factor that bridges every believer.
Jesus is the Redeemer the whole world needs, ransoming His life for unbelievers.

We may differ, but we share a commonwealth in Jesus, who is as humble as a servant.
We may differ and fall short toward another; this reminds us to be observant.
On the night He was betrayed, humble Jesus washed twelve pairs of feet.
He told others to do the same or else they wouldn't be in Him complete.
Believers should uphold with love and bear burdens for one another
When the daily grind of life hinders and new situations seem tougher.

Jesus is the chief cornerstone and common factor that bridges every believer.
Jesus is the Redeemer the whole world needs, ransoming His life for unbelievers.

We need to lift up and help others, not get after them; this not ours to muster.
We need to remind one another that with God, the Enemy is always outnumbered.
Elisha prayed, "Lord open my servant's eyes to see the heavenly host all around."
The Lord answered and will do the same for all loved ones being held bound.
Paul said everything will work out for the good to all who love God.
Those called for His purpose regardless of what potholes may be caused.

Jesus is the chief cornerstone and common factor that bridges every believer.
Jesus is the Redeemer the whole world needs, ransoming His life for unbelievers.

C+RAD

Poetry101 3X

There's no love greater than God alone, no one else that you will find.
His light pierced through the void of darkness, in this He has redefined.
His love is greater than parental love; this has taken on some changes
In a world that wrestles from a fallen nature and all false persuasions.

Sin produces rotten, diseased fruit that is spoiled and not good for the soul.
It works on the inside, destroying what's good and soon won't be whole.
Yet God has a purpose—to change all things from bad to very good
Especially when today's kids and teens grow up in a single parenthood.

This vain world is turning further away from truth and toward errors.
You see, the school system all around is hiring some very good storytellers.
The world revolves, still turning because it will only obey the Creator.
Coming soon: a system designed by greedy men giving liberty to an imitator.

Jesus awaits the call from His Father to go and take care of some business.
When the church is taken up, every believer gone from a world of dimness.
Sometimes logic can seem too far to reach, barely visible for all to see.
Jesus opened the eyes of blind Bartimaeus; He'll do the same for you and me.

C+RAD

PoetryIOI 3y

Heaven is a place where God resides, and a place for the redeemed.
Heaven is a place unmatched in beauty, a real place we all have dreamed.
Paul writes that to be absent from the body is to be present with the Lord.
We should have this desire as we partake in His Word and become reassured.
We may have dreamt of heaven in a form, although perhaps not understanding.
The Bible reveals God's view of heaven, providing us a better grasping.

Heaven is a place of happiness where no sinful man or deceiving angel resides.
Heaven is a place where the Son shines bright and the vile will remain outside.

A place of completeness and no more sorrows or sad tears of despair.
A place of rest where peace and joy sway in meadows, dancing together.
The Bible describes heaven as the final stop for all who have been redeemed—
A place of rest with innocence again and beauty beyond all we've ever dreamed,
Where time ceases to exist while completeness overtakes all evil demises,
Warranting eternal peace from the Son of God; this the Father promises.

Heaven is a place of happiness where no sinful man or deceiving angel resides.
Heaven is a place where the Son shines bright and the vile will remain outside.

A little bit of paradise maybe found on some tropical Island down here.
A little bit of sin can keep you from heaven and is something you shouldn't conceal.
Some areas this world has reflect bits of heaven; He made these for our amusement,
Bringing our heart back to welcome what He has created for our enjoyment.
Yes, a little bit of sin will keep anyone from entering heaven's paradise.
This the Devil would make you disbelieve, or else deal with his compromise.

Heaven is a place of happiness where no sinful man or deceiving angel resides.
Heaven is a place where the Son shines bright and the vile will remain outside.

C+RAD

PoetrylOl 32

There are sometimes you'll need to get away, just to be alone
So you can collect yourself and your reasoning; hey, turn off the iPhone.
The Son of God, Jesus, went alone to pray; this He practiced quite often.
Works and things, He'd meditate on from His Father to do and be spoken.

In the world full of natural and unnatural noises, we need times of refreshing.
We need time away from this in order to collect new thoughts in the making.
A three- or four-year-old car battery will show signs that it needs replacing.
Our character shows signs of phasing, and then it's time for some vacationing.

God took some time off and dedicated a day for a very good reason.
He knew we'd turn ourselves into slaves to cares and worldly treasons.
He took time off; let us follow His example and stop all compromising
In a world that has no regard for people, but word play and dehumanizing.

We came into this world for reasons directed from the one and only Creator.
The Devil will challenge you on this whether you're a true believer or unbeliever.
You need to know who you are and where you'll spend all of eternity.
The choice is yours; He knows all hearts desire to repent from all absurdity.

C+RAD

Poetry101

Never Full

Hell and destruction are never full,
Full without regard whether rich or poor,
Poor in spirit with a desire to be whole,
Whole and pure, as Christ assures with grandeur,
Grandeur in heart we shall have forevermore,
Forevermore with Jesus—no hassles anymore,
Nothing anymore; no aches or sorrows evermore.

C+RAD

Poetry101

A Lofty Fool

Wisdom is too lofty for a fool,
A fool that has nothing better to do
Than otherwise irritate or ridicule,
Ridicule things that are perfectly in view,
In view as wisdom clears away all hullabaloos,
All hullabaloos the Devil throws at me and you,
Everyone who desires Jesus and a life anew.

C+RAD

Poetry101

Daily Favor

Be zealous for the fear of the Lord all day,
All day He'll reassure you, no matter what comes your way.
The way is with Jesus not the 10, 60, or 91 freeway,
A freeway full of joy without erroneous leeway.
Leeway in life means we'll drift off when we won't obey,
Obey instructions from His Word and take time to pray,
Praying daily so that a heart and mind won't stray.

C+RAD

Poetry101

True Knowledge

The eyes of the Lord preserve true knowledge,
True knowledge the Lord Jesus has always promised,
Promised to all a brand-new covenant,
A new covenant changing dishonest hearts to honest.
Honest and ardent souls enter His harvest,
A harvest God the Father knows of, that's quite obvious,
As obvious as evil caught in its undergarments.

C+RAD

Poetry101

Our Strong Tower, Jesus

The name of the Lord is a very strong tower,
A strong tower lean and full of His power.
His power demons have seen every day, every hour.
Every hour, evil and darkness still try to overpower,
Overpower a world becoming twisted and sour,
So sour all evil is waiting to devour,
Devour for a short time till Jesus they encounter.

C+RAD

Poetry101

The House of God

Walk prudently when you go to the house of God,

God who is the Creator of heaven and earth and beyond,

Beyond galaxies and horizons, crossing every tittle and jot.

A jot so small like sin will always try to rob.

Rob, kill, and destroy the Devil will, if not on watch

To watch and pray for everyone Christ has surely touched,

Touching all sullen hearts and granting acceptance with a nod.

C+RAD

Poetry101

Godly Correction

Do not withhold correction from a child,
A child needing true guidance and to be heavenly reconciled,
Reconciled with no guile from godly parents that aspire,
Aspire from God the Father, whom we all need to admire.
Admire and compile our prayers that He'll surely inspire,
Inspire from His Son, Jesus, who will set many hearts afire,
And who's afire in dire need to lift empty hearts with a smile.

C+RAD

A Heart Well Applied

Apply your heart to His daily instructions,
His instructions and no more adverse presumptions,
Presumptions that can lead to different assumptions,
Assumptions without any manipulate deductions,
Deductions that aren't equal to any subtractions,
Subtractions that won't add up to any attractions,
Attractions that Christ brings with true satisfaction.

C+RAD

Poetry101

Patience

A patient spirit is better than a proud-minded spirit.
A proud spirit hinders prayers, making our walk very different,
Very different and far from our Savior, who is the Lord Jesus,
The Lord Jesus who came to save a world and totally free us,
Free us from pain and worldly stress causing much weariness,
Weariness and all sufferings Christ took upon Him to heal us,
Heal us from all wretched evil the Devil uses for his purpose.

C+RAD

A Generous Soul

A generous soul will be made rich,

Made rich from God's Word, known to enrich,

To enrich hearts for souls filling a void like a bridge,

A bridge Christ gave to a world hanging on a hinge,

A hinge opening longing hearts waiting for His heaven.

Heaven is a place without any evil aggressions,

Aggressions corrected upon Christ's wonderful redemption.

C+RAD

Poetry101

His Favor

A good man obtains favor from the Lord,
The Lord God Almighty—one to be adored,
Adored, yet obscured from our sin He took and absorbed,
Absorbed with His Father's love—this He performed,
Performed and restored all who will be forewarned.
Forewarn the Devil that he's about to be outsourced,
Outsourced with all evil when heaven and earth become transformed.

C+RAD

Poetry101

A Husband's Crown

An excellent wife is the crown of her husband,
Her husband, who is blessed by her love right offhand.
Right offhand, life will demand and try to disband,
Disband a marriage, but Jesus has the upper hand,
The upper hand in marriages broken and harassed,
Harassed by worldly cares the Devil has dispatched,
Dispatched then reattached by Christ's love unsurpassed.

C+RAD

Poetry101 4A

Comparing people to radio antennas, some differ or vary in frequency.
Comparing Christians in faith, some are strong or vary in delinquency.
Twelve disciples varied in faith; Jesus knew their hearts from the start.
He'll choose anyone, knowing a heart will still be so very marred.
We tend to acknowledge people more outwardly than from on the inside.
He's never distracted by appearances but by how the heart parallels and coincides.

Faith is the substance of things hoped for, by the evidence of things not seen.
Faith will vary with every believer, but it is God that reveals the unseen.

This is the beauty that God will work in the hearts of His redeemed.
This is the beauty when a believer testifies of hopes that have been retrieved,
Giving and taking truths from people's experiences some will doubt or behold.
In a city called Nazareth, Jesus wanted to bless as they criticized and condoned.
Faith is just as big as sin, even bigger, when your heart's tuned to embark.
Yes, faith has moved great obstacles in the lives of the great patriarchs.

Faith is the substance of things hoped for, by the evidence of things not seen.
Faith will vary with every believer, but it is God that reveals the unseen.

God will bring back lives of people that turn from an unrepentant heart.
God will bring back family and friends, seeing hearts desiring a new start.
Jacob's heart renewed when he heard Joseph was alive and well.
God's promises are like spring waters over flowing with health.
He'll defend and protect His children, as a shepherd will do for his sheep.
God separates the bad from good, as a farmer separates tares from the wheat.

Faith is the substance of things hoped for, by the evidence of things not seen.
Faith will vary with every believer, but it is God that reveals the unseen.

C+RAD

Poetry101 4B

Easter is a time of reflection in the lives of old and new believers
Celebrating the resurrection of Jesus the Christ, who's every believer's Savior.
Jesus is the Son of God, who gave His life as a ransom on a rugged cross.
The Devil, taking two steps backward, knew his time was soon to be lost.

God sent His only Son to redeem a crooked and perverted world,
A world He created spankin' new for a heavenly couple on reserve.
This couple took matters into their own hands and disobeyed His command,
A command that would cost both of them; thus the Father had to reprimand.

Now the choice is for everyone that would desire and want a new life,
This new life coming at full price, reviving a dead soul becoming alive.
Jesus the Christ, the spotless Lamb, was slain for a world lost in confusion.
His blood He shed on a wooden cross was the only way and true solution.

Time now running short and darkness all around ramping up quite fast,
This is a serious decision, and one that shouldn't make anyone laugh.
The only one who is laughing is the Devil, waiting for you to choose,
Thinking he has the upper hand in this and always wanting you to lose.

C+RAD

Poetry101 4C

The joy of the Lord is greater than Disneyland or any amusement park.
The joy of the Lord will take you to places you'd never dream to embark.
The joy this world gives is temporary, but the joy of the lord is eternal.
His grace will wrap you in royalty and His truth as authentic as purple.
King Solomon asked for wisdom and understanding to lead a great people.
God answered and will do the same to lead people from upheaval.

Yes, God is love and has endless satisfaction for a meek heart and soul.
Yes, God is love and wants all mankind to be free and made whole.

This is available for people wanting true direction and a brand-new life.
This also prepares new hearts to be forgiven and to rejoice for the afterlife.
John 14:6—Jesus gave three principles on how to proceed to the Father.
Yet in a mixed-up world, we'll try to misrepresent, making this look harder.
The Devil will try to abuse the law of liberty profound in God's Word,
Seeing many taken from his plan as the gospel brings life to all on the verge.

Yes, God is love and has endless satisfaction for a meek heart and soul.
Yes, God is love and wants all mankind to be free and made whole.

The life after this, if one is a Christian, will never, ever be boring.
Life now, if unchanged, will end in darkness and tears outpouring.
The two, compared, are like night and day when you put your trust in the Lord Jesus,
Putting back together your life that was messed up and strewn in so many pieces.
Time is at hand, and you don't know where you'll stand now or for all eternity.
Take the time now and be humble, not proud; ask Jesus in your heart today.

Yes, God is love and has endless satisfaction for a meek heart and soul.
Yes, God is love and wants all mankind to be free and made whole.

C+RAD

Poetry101 4D

"Raising Cain" is a play on words, and Cain's found in Genesis of the Bible.
Having sibling rivalries cost his brother Abel's life; this led to Cain's denial.
God knows the heart of every individual He still has compassion for.
You know that sin is crouched and waiting for you to open the door.

Trouble will have no problems finding you if you wave to all its fallacies.
People have many problems recognizing fakes among life's realities.
Becoming popular in today's culture are smart TVs, makin' people dumb,
Having their head wedged between their thighs, or maybe even their thumb

No problem having too much time on hand; just depends on time being spent,
Especially if one is an unbeliever and the Lord Jesus Christ isn't your friend.
You can be young or old, two peas in a pod, but with no salvation to show.
The Bible, God's Word written for you, is all you'll ever need to know.

Everyone has problems and troubles, or if they don't, then they're fibbing or lyin'.
Don't give up on life or the Creator of it, God; He'll know if you're really tryin'.
Put your trust in His only Son, Jesus; He's the one that is the only way.
A thief on the cross gave his life to Jesus; he's now living in paradise this day.

C+RAD

Poetry101 4E

Would you exemplify giving your life for something you truly believe in?
Would you give your life in exchange for another, no matter the cost therein?
Jesus changed the hearts and lives of twelve men He then made disciples.
Yes, they too would change a dead world that is quickly spiraling downward.
God has His plans set in motion that no one thought they'd be apart of.
The Godhead witnessed this at Christ's baptism in the form of a dove.

God sent His only Son, who gave His life for a world so lost in sin.
God sent His only Son, who did the job, shedding His blood for all, amen.

Jesus, the Lamb of God, sacrificed His life for a darkened world.
Jesus is God incarnate, the Great I AM, and the soon-coming King returned.
Jesus is the one true sacrifice who cleanses all sinners from the grip of sin.
This happens as you give your heart to Him, and the changes will soon begin
Jesus is coming to pick up a people that are redeemed by His precious blood.
We'll bow down to Jesus the King with our heart greatly becoming touched.

God sent His only Son, who gave His life for a world so lost in sin.
God sent His only Son, who did the job, shedding His blood for all, amen.

God has abundant love for everyone and judgment for unruly people
God loves saving souls from evil and every heart from becoming too deceitful.
There's no greater love than God's in sending His Son to die for us on the cross.
The Devil thought he had a win, but this event turned out to be a total loss.
In the end it'll make a difference if you're a sinner becoming a true believer.
The Devil wants many people deceived while becoming the one big loser.

God sent His only Son, who gave His life for a world so lost in sin.
God sent His only Son, who did the job, shedding His blood for all, amen.

C+RAD

Poetry101 4F

The Easter bunny is sure to bring goodies to many kids all around,
Bringing joy and happiness by hopping to places where kids can be found.
The Easter bunny brings many of his friends to help give baskets full of treats
Baskets full of brightly colored Easter eggs and candies so good to eat.

The Easter bunny always dresses nice for this fun and very special occasion,
Hopping near Snow White's house and sharing a basket for the huntsman.
The Easter bunny's friends finally arrive to gather the baskets and help out—
Friends like duck, owl, deer, squirrel, and gopher—all one big turnout.

Every year, the crowds of kids grow more and more in such abundance,
Letting the Easter bunny know how many baskets are needed for the next adjustment.
The Easter bunny and friends are so happy, knowing they're bringing joy continually
As the Easter bunny and friends hand out many baskets in God's grace so tenderly.

Whether or not you believe or not in an Easter bunny, believe in Jesus the Christ,
God's only beloved Son, who died on a Roman cross to set free and revive.
This is not close to being a fairy tale, what Jesus did to heal a sick world—
A world He would give His life for at a price; His Father looked down and confirmed.

C+RAD

Poetry101 4G

The whole world was at a loss before Jesus took our place on the cross.
The whole world gave into sin, becoming tattered and torn with many flaws.
Jesus comforted His sheep; He's known as the true Good Shepherd.
He's prayin' for young and old believers the Devil wants completely severed.
Jesus is known to touch many hearts becoming lost or at times distracted
When cares of this world overtake and keep our minds so disenchanted.

There's no excuse in not turning your heart to Jesus the Savior.
There's no excuse, yet many will die in their unchanged sinful nature.

Technology and pride: you'll need to keep watch or they'll ruin your life.
Technology and pride: too much of either one will become a dominating vice.
Technology and pride are used to drive us to accomplish good things in life,
A life that is very fast paced and given at a huge, demanding price.
Don't let these two try to make you look like or become such a fool.
The Devil will always try your character, or maybe even ridicule you.

There's no excuse in not turning your heart to Jesus the Savior.
There's no excuse yet, many will die in their unchanged sinful nature.

Man turns to technology for answers that only God has and by choice will share.
Man turns away from God by choice, with the Devil's ploys becoming a snare.
God has all the answers, of course; He's the Creator of everything,
While man is still in a fallen nature and has a brain the size of a pea.
Man is still dealing with pride, like the Devil, and this is not becoming good.
God sent His Son, sending the Devil on the run; we now have a better livelihood.

There's no excuse in not turning your heart to Jesus the Savior.
There's no excuse, yet many will die in their unchanged sinful nature.

C+RAD

Poetryl0l 4H

Are you downright grateful to God, who sent His Son for a cause?
The cause was that lives were at the mercy of the Devil's many repertoires.
His Son's name is Jesus or Savior, the anointed one, who was and is to come.
He was born to die to liberate and set free a world becoming very glum.

A star in the sky, signifying His birth, heralded the King of Kings
As shepherds watched into the night, while angels proclaimed many things.
He grew in favor with God and man, bringing delight to a Devilish world.
He taught twelve ordinary fishermen by trade; thus His Father approved.

Jesus proclaimed His Father's teachings, bringing healings to many people,
Touching the lives of people lame, blind, or mute and oppressed with evil.
A sect of religious people zealous of dead works, pressing the people of God,
Became like the people Jesus would heal, only putting on a slithery facade.

Judas, one of the twelve disciples, betrayed Jesus for thirty pieces of silver.
A religious sect had Jesus crucified, not knowing this was planned by His Father.
God had designed a plan in bringing salvation to a world coming undone,
A plan designed for an unspotted lamb to shed its blood, this by Jesus, His Son.

C+RAD

PoetryIOI 4i

I am reminded daily how much God has blessed me in His Word.
I am reminded daily of His counsels of old, keeping my heart ready and stirred.
Just as our body needs exercise, the same is true of our mind and heart.
Dedicating time for His Father's words, Jesus applied this from the very start.
It takes a desire to apply sound doctrine daily and also to walk unselfishly.
Jesus applied this on the cross, giving His life for all immoral infidelity.

God sweeps away the sorrows and cares of this world from meddling.
God keeps a heart and mind tuned to His grace from ever despairing.

He lovingly cares in keeping us free from strongholds and mindless clutter.
He lovingly cares in keeping our heart from speaking anything harmful or vulgar.
Jesus became very angry at all the religious sect's countless treasons.
This religious sect made up false claims about Jesus for all the wrong reasons.
He was beaten and marred beyond recognition, yet He died for all that day,
Paying a debt He did not owe, and all of us owing a debt we couldn't pay.

God sweeps away the sorrows and cares of this world from meddling.
God keeps a heart and mind tuned to His grace from ever despairing.

God loves a heart to be carefree and full of His wonderful loving-kindness.
God loves a heart to be free from this world's horrific mindlessness.
Let not your heart be troubled with many cares and worries that surely stifle.
You'll find soundness and edification when you make time to read the Bible.
God cares for each person regardless of their past, present, or future sin.
God wants everyone's heart free of sin, starting brand-new from within.

God sweeps away the sorrows and cares of this world from meddling.
God keeps a heart and mind tuned to His grace from ever despairing.

C+RAD

PoetrylOl 4j

Grace is not just a name for a person or an expression for charm and beauty.
This happened two thousand years ago, taking place as the world became a tad gloomy.
When the fullness of time came, God sent His Son to a world filled with shame.
Shame came from a fallen nature, which man took upon and then became.

This fallen nature man chose, and then he was deceived by a trick of a fool,
A fool who is well known as the Devil, or the deceiver, wanting always to overrule.
God gave man complete dominion, rule over all God had created and made.
Man fell short of a royal flush because he chose wrong and then disobeyed.

God has love and favor for all; this is called God's wonderful grace.
This grace is demonstrated by His Son, Jesus, whom we're all told to embrace.
There are many things this world offers to embrace but only are temporary.
His grace for us brings liberty to a world ready to treat anyone unfairly.

The grace of God is beyond our understanding, which graces all of his reasoning,
While grace is an attribute of a holy God, making man feel only inconveniencing.
Grace is a wonderful gift from God to man that has no strings attached.
The Devil will try his best at keeping your heart and mind very handicapped.

C+RAD

PoetryIOI 4K

Jesus is the Son of God sent by His Father with love from above.
Jesus is one whom every father would be amazed and surely very proud of.
Jesus grew in favor with God and man, his parents guided by a heavenly plan.
The world would soon learn that He would grow up as no ordinary man.
Mary, like a mother, would care for all her children and her husband Joseph.
These parents gave love to all their children while directing, without any what-ifs.

Joseph, Mary's husband, lived a life that God blessed very amiably.
Joseph, Mary's husband, lived very humbly with so much modesty.

God knows people will differ in their character and have hearts not very mindful.
God knows people have a sinful nature and a heart not very grateful.
God is ready to put joy back in hearts and lift upside-down people up again.
He also wants all to turn to His Son, Jesus, who sticks closer as a friend.
God also knows hearts can change overnight in favor with a heavenly recipe.
Love, peace, joy, happiness, and a tender heart He'll give to you and me.

Joseph, Mary's husband, lived a life that God blessed very amiably.
Joseph, Mary's husband, lived very humbly with so much modesty.

God uses people with simple minds and lives that became very broken.
God uses people with lives in motion and tender hearts ready to be outspoken.
The natural mind and sinful heart will do only what they want to do.
This can become very troubling and is not the right course to pursue.
God can use someone who is willing to become outspoken for the gospel truths,
Turning a world back from relativity, thinking of all of God's absolutes.

Joseph, Mary's husband, lived a life that God blessed very amiably.
Joseph, Mary's husband, lived very humbly with so much modesty.

C+RAD

PoetryI0I 4L

The love of God and His grace is in the front of all beloved believers.
Godless and meaningless things are behind for all the doggy retrievers.
Living daily in God's grace is the believer's assurance that He truly cares.
God always cares for His people who share and converse in daily prayers.

Thank God for His blessings, which keep a heart above troubled waters.
Especially when the world believes in UFOs and alien flying saucers.
God's grace is always available, even if a hardened world is a bit of a trifle.
Going across the grain in life can sometimes become spitefully frightful.

We are the apple of His eye, while He's the great pearl of great price.
The way to the Father is through His Son, Jesus, taking us to His paradise.
Grace is also caring for others regardless of the nature of the beast.
Mercy and grace come from His Son and from knowing His Father is well pleased.

So for every believer in Jesus the Savior, grace is always in the front of us.
Wickedness and Devilish deeds are behind, or in the back of a yellow bus.
Walk daily in God's wonderful grace through Jesus, His only Son,
who bestows loving grace upon us so that our lives can surely be fun.

C+RAD

Poetry101 4M

God's standards of living are high—higher than the heavens could contain.
God's standards of living: we chose wrong, and the tree brought the pain.
Adam and Eve disobeyed God, eating fruit from the Tree of Good and Evil
This happens when discernment's off-kilter and prayers to seek Him are needful.
God's standards aren't cumbersome; it's the sin manifested against the law.
The law shows it's the sin that gives everyone those human natural flaws.

God is holy and requires praises from our heart and not from unclean lips.
God is holy and will curtail all the Devil's schemes that can and will surely trip.

God gave His best to all of mankind in sending His beloved Son, Jesus.
God gave His Spirit to all believers and changed our hearts in saving us.
He gave His best not because of the wrong, but because His love transcends.
His love transcends from the very beginning and will never have any ends.
He promised His Spirit will guide and direct us all; yes, this is very true.
The Holy Spirit's purpose is to help and equips all believers with tools to use.

God is holy and requires praises from our heart and not from unclean lips.
God is holy and will curtail all the Devil's schemes that can and will surely trip.

The Word of God speaks on love and a fondness for all unselfish hearts
The Word, if read and enjoyed daily, will keep a heart from wanting to depart
The Bible helps build believers spiritual stances this morning, noon and night
His Word will defend a believer's heart and made ready in the spirits might
We're to pray and not grow tired, in the cares and worries of worldly squabbles
A world ran by many demons yet God encourages not to be buried in troubles

God is holy and requires praises from our heart and not from unclean lips.
God is holy and will curtail all the Devil's schemes that can and will surely trip.

C+RAD

Poetry101 4N

The Bible is the best book about parenting, one that shares hopes from failures—
Failures that are from different behaviors and also have some fruity flavors.
Parenting is God's best feature and one that Adam and Eve messed up forever,
Especially when one is talking to a snake and believing all its unethical answers.

Parenting is definitely a challenge, and one that requires constant prayers—
Prayers that arise within our faith to a holy God who beholds and cares,
Prayers that also stimulate a heart and many tears flowing from His grace.
Come before an all-knowing and -seeing God who will take us to a higher place.

When it comes down to knowledge and how to handle problems, God is always there.
He'll be there when things seem to go wrong and stuff becomes not very clear.
Parenting is being candid and true even when life bellows right in your face,
Something God is well aware of because the world He created shuns His grace.

So remember, parenting is a daily necessity and one that reaps many blessings—
Blessings from God the Father and His Son, Jesus, keeping us from all complaining.
This is where the Bible comes in to muster and cater to all wants or needs.
The need to bring blessings is felt while parenting as the Holy Spirit guides and leads.

C+RAD

Poetry101 40

The glory of the Lord shone as a very dark cloud that appeared on Mt. Sinai.
The glory of the Lord: Jesus is the glory of His Father that truly shines brightly.
The children of God feared the glory that shone quite dark on Mt. Sinai.
God told Moses to keep the people from the mountain or else they would die.
God the Creator is holy and true; yet the Devil will always tell you no.
That He's holy and will not stand in sin's presence, who doesn't know?

Jesus gave His disciples glimpses of His Father's heavenly glory.
Jesus the beloved Son of God—His Father spoke of His Son's authority.

God expressed love for His Son and all His Son would do for Him.
God expressed love for believers in His Son while helping and guiding them.
Jesus expressed love for His Father and the sacrifice He was sent to do.
Humbling himself as a lamb for reconciliation, this He did for me and you.
Jesus never had second thoughts of the plan His Father had to save mankind.
The Devil thought it was over for mankind, yet God kept him very mesmerized.

Jesus gave His disciples glimpses of His Father's heavenly glory.
Jesus the beloved Son of God—His Father spoke of His Son's authority.

God has compassion through His Son, Jesus, for all unadjusted hearts.
God has the power over evil to readjust hearts and those wanting to depart.
Hardened clad hearts may try to eclipse all the counsels of God regrettably,
Only to realize they're jeopardizing their souls and lives for all eternity.
Never shake a fist at a holy and compassionate God who will never snap.
He's all-loving and caring, even to anyone who ends up looking like a sap.

Jesus gave His disciples glimpses of His Father's heavenly glory.
Jesus the beloved Son of God—His Father spoke of His Son's authority.

C+RAD

Poetry101 4P

Poetry writing will vary, depending upon where you or your mind is or isn't.
It's like playing some old board games, like Candy Land or maybe Kiss Mint.
In poetry you decide on what you're willing to share or just even makeup.
Makeup something funny or maybe something straight from the dump.

Okay, so you have your thoughts and all that you're willing to say.
Now go ahead and put this together in a poem that grabs them, okay?
It never hurts to have a dictionary or a thesaurus that's nearby.
As you put words and many thoughts together, you let out a sigh.

Wow, the many hours or so; your heart and mind have been at it ever since.
Now, realizing only a few words are written, you're really starting too wince.
Yes, it can be a real challenge, but hey, that's what life's all about.
It's about having some fun while tryin' your best and not wearing yourself out.

God has a purpose for every person, regardless of many situations.
Regarding everyone's situations in life, sin is the reason for the separation.
He's a loving Creator who knows all our wants and many needs,
Especially sending His beloved Son to save a world from its many misdeeds.

C+RAD

Poetry101 40

It's not over when many dreams, goals, or promises just seem to fly by.
It's not over when God has the final say, and on Him we need to rely.
God makes promises, and He sure has never broken any of them at all—
Promises, not compromises—and all this is written in His Word overall
He keeps His part while we lag on our end when doubt or fear draws near.
He gently gives us a little nudge in His Spirit to humble ourselves in prayer.

God has lined up for unsettled setbacks in a believer's life His plentiful paybacks.
God has abundant blessings for us, replacing the Devil's harassments and attacks.

Abel's blood spoke out to God for justice on what his brother Cain had done.
Christ's blood spoke out to His Father on what His redemption had forever won.
The power in the blood of Jesus won liberty and free reign for every believer.
His shed blood for you and I will save and set free all unruly unbelievers.
This is spoken out to a lost world in such dire need of His great godly love,
Unconditional love reserved for changed unbelievers—all this from God above.

God has lined up for unsettled setbacks in a believer's life His plentiful paybacks.
God has abundant blessings for us, replacing the Devil's harassments and attacks.

The light of the gospel is coming soon; Jesus awaiting His Father's call.
The light of the gospel's sovereign call says the Devil's reign is about to fall.
The outcome of the end has already been foretold from the very beginning.
In the beginning, the Devil deceived two innocents into conspiratorial sinning.
God told the serpent, "He shall bruise your head, and you shall bruise His heel."
Jesus on the cross cried out to the Father, "It is finished and done with the ordeal."

God has lined up for unsettled setbacks in a believer's life His plentiful paybacks.
God has abundant blessings for us, replacing the Devil's harassments and attacks.

C+RAD

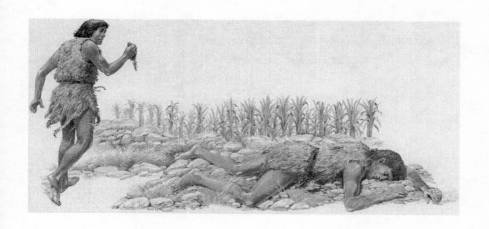

Poetry101 4R

Every believer's standing with God never changes, even with many mistakes.
Mistakes He sees, but in His Son Jesus, His shed blood gave us a break.
This standing, which God gracefully gave to us from His only beloved Son,
Would, without Christ in your life, certainly weigh much more than a ton.

Now each person has a state of being, whether a true believer or not.
This state of being could change, such as Adam's and Eve's when they got caught.
Doing wrong changes hearts and minds needing emptying into a Dumpster.
This happens when struggles in life take bites out of our own luster.

When you're redeemed in Christ Jesus, God then sees that you're really clean—
Clean inside the heart, with the light of the gospel shining; know what I mean?
God is thrilled at what His Son has done for a lost and turbulent world.
So lost was the Devil, celebrating only to find the curse was overturned.

So your standing in God will judge daily your state of mind.
Your state of mind will change from just the drop of a dime.
Remember, God sees no sin in us because of Jesus, His only Son,
Our Savior who died on a rugged cross with love for everyone.

C+RAD

Poetry101 4S

In our weaknesses we're made strong; this is God's true handiwork.
In our weaknesses He'll elevate us when demises are flying off the hook.
Grace and strength are available when we're without hope and very weak.
But strength is made complete in Jesus when things are lookin' very bleak.
Praise God in weaknesses that Christ's power may indwell within us—
Yes, everyone who has put their faith and trust in His Son, the Lord Jesus.

God is very gracious when it comes to comforting and applying His sympathy.
God is very gracious when it comes to showing His patience toward us so amiably.

Give praise to God for being wonderful in all aspects of a believer's life.
Give praise to God for eternal life we find in His Son, Jesus the Christ.
Let everything that has breath praise the Lord and again praise the Lord.
He has given to all of us eternal life that is so miraculously restored
As we lift the name of Jesus in the good times and also through the bad.
The bad He changes for us with grace when we're at times becoming very sad.

God is very gracious when it comes to comforting and applying His sympathy.
God is very gracious when it comes to showing His patience toward us so amiably.

For those not knowing His amazing grace and the salvation plan from His Son;
For those thinking that life exists as is, with complacent minds becoming far gone;
When we were still without strength, in due time Christ died for the ungodly—
The ungodly thinking, standing in their own fate, all gaudy and very gawky.
In one man's shame, death reigned, but now by God's gift of grace we're justified—
Justified when His love supersedes our complacent minds now becoming purified.

God is very gracious when it comes to comforting and applying His sympathy.
God is very gracious when it comes to showing His patience toward us so amiably.

C+RAD

Poetry101 4T

The cross of Christ brought death and true redemption from sin—
Sin coming from within the garden of Eden, from a dark, slithery villain.
This villain, also known as the Devil, knowingly deceived two people.
These people disobeyed a command and ran from a heavenly steeple.

So don't point fingers at anyone when three are pointing back at the accuser.
This Devil knew and had fun with this ultimate, brand-spankin'-new maneuver.
He is also known as being very cunning and shining as an angel of light.
His light he uses to deceive people, making wrong things look very right.

The light of days is growing dark, and this world is sure caught in the mess,
A mess that grows from worldly minds not truly wanting to profess,
Profess that this world needs dire help; if only they would drop to a knee—
A knee showing humbleness and all hearts wanting to become surely free.

The answer to a world of problems is found in the beginning of this poem—
The Son of God, Christ Jesus, bringing a world back, becoming very wholesome.
Yes, He's the only answer that this darkened world is truly in dire need of.
He'll be coming back very soon, and everyone will see Jesus coming from above.

C+RAD

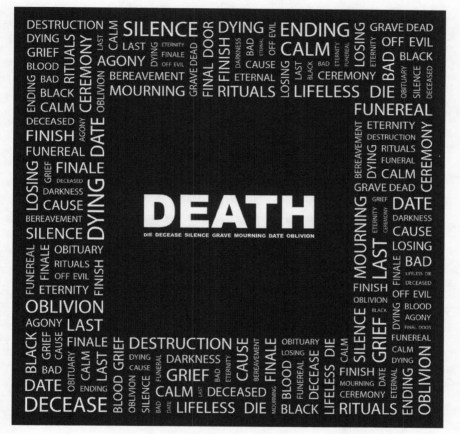

Poetry101 4U

The environment and climate are rapidly changing for some very bad reasons.
The environment and climate are tired of dealing with secular and ungodly heathens.
The Devil is the reason for the chaotic changes in and around the world.
A world of greedy people depleting resources are not very concerned.
Their concern is for the reasons that wrong people don't really care a lot
when governments are out to lunch and eventually will get caught.

A world created by a heavenly Creator and only to be ruined by an imitator,
This world was created by a triune Godhead who will always be the Originator.

This imitator is a fraudulent deceiver who makes bad things look good.
This imitator's pride was found in him who then chose a bad livelihood.
This imitator loves attention, and he'll do anything to try to get yours
And that of anyone else whose life shows signs of becoming very bored.
People grow bored with their lives when a heart turns stale with no spiritual continuity.
Their humanly hearts turn recklessly toward a life of sexual promiscuity.

A world created by a heavenly Creator and only to be ruined by an imitator,
This world was created by a triune Godhead who will always be the Originator.

This world was destroyed by a great flood, and all this was in His merciful plans.
This world will be destroyed by a great fire; this we need to understand.
The world that then existed perished by being flooded because of ungodly men.
God loved these ungodly men even when they continued doing wrong again.
In the heavens and earth of old, God's Word stood firm and very true
Yet reserved for fire, judgment, and hell was this—a world untrue.

A world created by a heavenly Creator and only to be ruined by an imitator,
This world was created by a triune Godhead who will always be the Originator.

C+RAD

Poetry101 4V

The Devil, or the accuser of the brethren, confuses many modern-day churches
Who fight among each other over worthless, trivial manmade jargons.
This is true, yet we need to remind ourselves daily who the real Enemy is:
The Devil, who will kill, steal, and destroy; who slithers around having an evil hiss.

This evil hiss he has used to confuse many believers not very literate in the gospel—
A gospel he'll twist for his own use to make many believers become very hostile.
We're to remember as believers never to use our own strength when called to fight.
We fight by prayer and waiting upon the Holy Spirit to direct, lead, and truly guide.

He is also known to imitate a roaring lion walking about, and to intimidate
All who put their trust in a loving God who's known to freely liberate.
Listen, until all believers realize he's the real reason for all the naughty messes
Many countries will continue reforming and slowly becoming very godless.

The Devil will go down fighting, knowing he's defeated and taking all he's blinded.
People choosing the wide path leading to death, he has misguided.
Yes, he's also known as the god of this world, a world that he has truly degraded.
And so it is until God sends His only Son to liberate all people He has created.

C+RAD

PoetryIOI 4W

Good and evil are two peas from a pod that will surely be opposites.
Good and evil have differing approaches in life, but only one is opulent.
The good comes from God sending His only Son to a world not really caring,
Where evil and blame come from the Devil, making life too overbearing.
God sees what evil the Devil now uses to control worldly people,
Whose hearts are darkened with souls and characters very unequal.

Good couldn't come from the evil; nor will evil come from the good.
Good is what God called each day He created, but evil is always an unlikelihood.

The Tree of Good and Evil existed in the garden for only selfish reasons.
The Tree of Life was also in the garden to bring us toward His meekness.
Evil came from an angel who changed his mind, wanting the spotlight on him,
This because pride makes him believe he's the owner of heaven and everything.
Everything God created is despised by this evil angel, also known as a compromiser.
Furthermore, he's also known to many believers as a bad-mouthed criticizer.

Good couldn't come from the evil; nor will evil come from the good.
Good is what God called each day He created, but evil is always an unlikelihood.

God is 100 percent love, and this He displayed when He sent His beloved Son.
God is sold out for a world He created, telling sin, "Now you're truly outdone."
Whom are you sold out to, an evil compromiser or God's only true Son, Jesus?
One was created, and the other has always existed beyond time past reason,
A time that never existed, but was only He who is known as the Alpha and Omega.
Compared to a pint-sized diva, God is and will always be unanimously bigger.

Good couldn't come from the evil; nor will evil come from the good.
Good is what God called each day He created, but evil is always an unlikelihood.

C+RAD

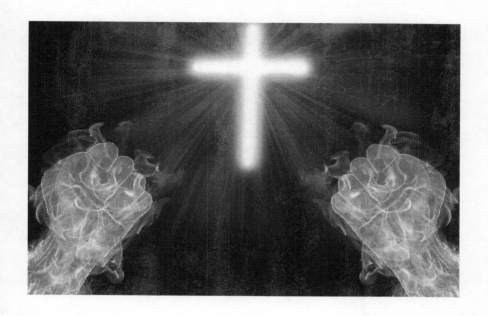

Poetry101 4X

This world glamorizes winning monies that would make anyone terribly green,
Very green; only a leprechaun would blush red, if you know what I mean.
The lotto, Powerball and various casinos want you to spend plenty of money
Which you've earned all your life and take your chances at becoming quite lucky.

Radio, TV, and iPhones advertise that if you don't play then you won't ever win
On gambling your monies away, which is also considered a covetous sin.
This sin, which the world considers only minor, is not about this bet thing ever.
I'm not hurting anyone if my lifestyle's that of a promiscuous fornicator

Money or becoming rich isn't all what life and the world is all about, you know.
Life can become funny or sad and then leave you with nothin' really to show,
Showing you it's not the bucks or Lady Luck that makes anyone feel really good.
No one but God is good; this is written in the Bible and not truly understood.

God is certainly the Creator of life, which was abundantly pure and simple
until, that is, man became so daring that he became sinful and very fickle.
God always had a plan that would save a world so lost at a tremendous cost—
A cost His Son would gladly bear for all: our shame upon a rugged cross.

C+RAD

Poetry101 4y

Life, as you know, can be a day-to-day challenge with its many struggles.
Life, as you know, without Jesus seems like most unsolved puzzles.
Jesus, the great problem solver, puts back together the lives of so many people.
For those needing a touch of God or encouraging words, this could be needful—
As needful as food baskets, financial help, or just some clothing to get by.
By only God's grace and His mercy do unsaved souls want to draw nigh.

To have Jesus in your life, it's like a well that will never run dry.
To have Jesus in your life, it's like heaven that's already nearby.

Knowing heavenly love that God has for us and reading the Bible daily
Knowing His Words bring much comfort to a world so mundanely
A world staggering at unprofitable knowledge when God has all the answers
Answers from a book called the Bible, with 66 books that He knows will matter
Each book having stories of many lives', that we all could really learn from
From God's point of view as we embraced sin our brain became surely dumb

To have Jesus in your life, it's like a well that will never run dry.
To have Jesus in your life, it's like heaven that's already nearby.

God lovingly wants a relationship with people wanting a clean heart.
God lovingly wants to heal every heart that sin made terribly marred.
People have many friends or relationships with various people out in the world,
which is full of taboos on loving the same gender as this thing spirals downward.
God is the answer to a world of problems and hearts needing His tender touch,
A touch no one could ever come close to but by Jesus, who loves us so much.

To have Jesus in your life, it's like a well that will never run dry.
To have Jesus in your life, it's like heaven that's already nearby.

C+RAD

PoetryIOl 4Z

This is a poem dedicated to people who do not know the Lord.
Our Lord is from the tribe of Judah and truly knows how to roar.
He roars as a lion does because he knows he's the King of Kings.
A King Jesus truly is, and the Creator of you, me, and everything.

People say they don't know the Lord, yet He knows all of them.
All of them He knows and loves, but sin ruins their lives and condemns
Their souls and hearts, which the Lord sees are in need of a fix.
He fixes many lives the Devil would love to see caught in his dark abyss.

God is a jealous god who hates any form of idolatrous living.
Idolatrous living makes God only a substitute, this is surely forbidden.
It is forbidden because there are no other gods, yet people make and create them,
All of them out of pride, which is a sin, and God says this time and time again.

The point is, God sent His only Son, Jesus, to save a very messy world.
The Devil messed this world up in disguising sin, so ownership is now transferred
From Adam to a deceiver, the Devil, thinking he's really the real thing.
The real thing is that Jesus died on a wooden cross for a world worth saving.

C+RAD

PoetryIOI

Find Wisdom

He who finds wisdom loves his own soul,
A soul in need of kindness when feelin' low.
When low, life will put you in a hole,
Leaving you tryin' not to lose self-control.
Self-control we all need more of, don't you know?
Don't you know bad and evil things the Devil will throw
at God-loving people with hearts of Jesus they'll show?

C+RAD

Poetry101

The Truth

Buy the truth and sell it not,
Not even if it cost you a lot.
But for now it's just some afterthought,
An afterthought caught in one's heart,
A heart needing a change from the start,
A start God wants dearly to be apart,
Apart as when a heart became truly marred.

C+RAD

Poetry101

Wisdom and Understanding

Does not wisdom cry and understanding lift up her voice?
Her voice the Lord lauds abundantly for all to hear and enjoy.
He enjoys His simplicity when cares of the world tend to annoy.
Annoyance, ploy, and decoy:these the Devil will use to destroy.
He destroys lives of godly people who have compassion, love, and joy,
A joy only God gives through His only Son Jesus, which we'll all enjoy
that day when we're all in heaven, whether man, woman, girl, or boy.

C+RAD

Poetry101

The Way of a Fool

The way of a fool is right in his eyes,
Eyes advising wrong choices that truly blind,
Blind eyes that nowise surmise or eventually theorize.
Nor do they criticize all absolutes God personifies.
God, who signifies with no compromise.
Compromise will deny godly insights that truly guide,
Guiding anyone accepting the Lord Jesus in their lives.

C+RAD

Poetry101

Direct Steps

A man's heart plans his way, but the Lord directs his steps.

His steps the Lord guides, and godly wisdom he accepts.

Accepting his neglect, the Lord knows and corrects.

He corrects everyone He loves at His own expense.

He does this for a world full of corrupt offences.

Offences will suppress truth, leading to many obsessions.

From obsessions He defends His beloved in prayer intercessions.

C+RAD

Poetry101

A Prudent Wife

A prudent wife is truly from the Lord,
The Lord God Almighty, steadfast and bold.
God is very bold; on His atonement He evoked.
He drove away evil intentions the Devil bestowed
Upon His Son Jesus'holy power to the utmost.
The utmost power Jesus gave everyone; His Father proposed
All hope, love, and eternal life for all He'll come to unfold.

C+RAD

Poetry101

Hatred and Love

Hatred stirs up strife, but love covers a multitude of sins.
All sin God has forgiven everyone of through His Son, Jesus,
Who died for a world caught up in a religious mess.
In this world of a mess, the Devil pressed people to transgress.
Transgression affects a mind and heart; that only Jesus can surely fix.
He fixes unhappy or saddened lives gripped by their own addicts.
Addicts and misfits God gladly directs to His beloved Son, Jesus.

C+RAD

Poetry101

The Tongue

Death and life are in the power of the tongue,
Which is able to spit out right things or wrong.
Wrong things dampen hearts, becoming weak, not strong.
Not being strong in faith makes our character run lukewarm.
Lukewarmness Christ scorns while willing hearts He transforms.
He does this unconditionally; the Father has earth adorned,
Adorned forever with our Savior, Jesus Christ, the Lord.

C+RAD

Poetry101

A Poor Man

He who loves pleasures becomes a poor man,
A poor man who's without God's true heavenly plan,
A plan going way back to when time first began.
It first began when man became such a sinful man,
So sinful and unruly he didn't even give a ram.
A ram or lamb without blemish is God's chosen plan,
A chosen plan helping mankind into God's wonderful clan.

C+RAD

Poetry101

The Lord God Is Our Maker

The rich and poor have this in common: the Lord God is their maker.
He is the maker of heaven and earth, the Lord Jesus Christ, the Savior.
The Savior gave His life as ransom for a world lost, a true lifesaver
Saving souls from the bondage maker, the Devil, a troublemaker.
Troubled people put their faith in Jesus, also known as the Mediator.
Jesus stands inbetween His Father and unrighteous people who are sinners.
Sinners put their trust in Jesus, who removes their worldly misbehaviors.

C+RAD

Poetry101

Eyes That Aren't Wise

Do not be wise in your own eyes,
Eyes reflecting a character that personifies,
Personifies right or wrong appetites,
Appetites that otherwise will scrutinize,
Scrutinize true love from Jesus the Christ.
Christ, God's only Son, He has immortalized.
He immortalized His loving sacrifice that truly sanctifies.

C+RAD

Poetry101

Path of the Wicked

Do not enter the path of the wicked,
The wicked with evil hearts already twisted,
Twisted with evil minds and completely infested.
They are infested, yet by God's grace evil is omitted,
Omitted by the sacrifice His Son has committed,
Committed by the shedding of blood God then quickened.
He quickly acquitted us of our sins when Christ was smitten.

C+RAD

Made in the USA
Las Vegas, NV
30 November 2021

35626643R00136